Constructing t

Constructing THE *Political Spectacle*

MURRAY EDELMAN

THE UNIVERSITY OF CHICAGO PRESS
CHICAGO AND LONDON

MURRAY EDELMAN is professor of political science at
the University of Wisconsin, Madison. Among his
previous books are *The Symbolic Uses of Politics* (1964);
Politics as Symbolic Action: Mass Arousal and Acquiescence
(1971); and *Political Language: Words That Succeed and
Policies That Fail* (1977).

The University of Chicago Press, Chicago 60637
The University of Chicago Press, Ltd., London

© 1988 by The University of Chicago
All rights reserved. Published 1988
Printed in the United States of America

97 96 95 94 93 92 91 90 89 88   5 4 3 2 1

Chapter 2 appeared in the *University of Miami Law Review*
42 (September 1987).

Library of Congress Cataloging-in-Publication Data

Edelman, Murray J. (Murray Jacob), 1919–
    Constructing the political spectacle.

    Includes index.
    1. Political psychology.   2. Symbolism in
politics.   3. Sociolinguistics.   4. United States—
Social conditions—1980–   I. Title.
JA74.5.E39   1988   320'.01'9   87-16239
ISBN 0-226-18397-1
ISBN 0-226-18399-8 (pbk.)

Contents

Acknowledgments

Just as the political spectacle is a construction, so is an author; my largest debts are owed to writers, teachers, and students who helped shape this book by constructing me, even if they are not cited. The colleagues who shaped it more directly through their trenchant criticisms of all or parts of the manuscript include Lance Bennett, James Farr, Martha Fineman, Gerda Lerner, Michael Lipsky, Cathy May, Richard Merelman, Martha Minow, Laurel Munger, Rozann Rothman, and Virginia Sapiro.

A John Simon Guggenheim Fellowship furnished support for my first book on political symbolism in the sixties, and a second Guggenheim Fellowship provided some of the time to write this one, as did a grant from the University of Wisconsin Research Board.

As a student of political language and symbolism, I am indebted in a different way to the countless public officials and representatives of political causes who spend their time giving me more data than I want, much of it disturbing or outrageous.

Lori Schlinkert and Renee Gibson inscribed the manuscript on floppy disks and revised it competently and patiently.

1 *Some Premises about Politics*

The pervasiveness of literacy, television, and radio in the industrialized world makes frequent reports of political news available to most of the population, a marked change from the situation that prevailed until approximately the Second World War. What consequences for ideology, action, and quiescence flow from preoccupation with political news as spectacle? How does the spectacle generate interpretations? What are its implications for democratic theory? Those are the questions addressed in this book.

There is a conventional answer that can be captured in a sentence rather than a volume: citizens who are informed about political developments can more effectively protect and promote their own interests and the public interest. That response takes for granted a world of facts that have a determinable meaning and a world of people who react rationally to the facts they know. In politics neither premise is tenable, a conclusion that history continually reaffirms and that observers of the political scene are tempted to ignore. To explore that conclusion is not likely to generate an optimistic book or a reassuring view of the human condition; but I hope this book will provide a realistic appreciation of the link between politics and well-being and a greater chance that political action can be effective.

The spectacle constituted by news reporting continuously constructs and reconstructs social problems, crises, enemies, and leaders and so creates a succession of threats and reassurances. These constructed problems and personalities furnish the content of political journalism and the data for historical and analytic political studies. They also play a central role in winning support and opposition for political causes and policies.

The latter role is usually masked by the assumption that citizens, journalists, and scholars are observers of "facts" whose meanings can be accurately ascertained by those who are properly trained and motivated. That positivist view is accepted rather than defended today. We are acutely aware that observers and what they observe construct one other; that political develop-

1

ments are ambiguous entities that mean what concerned observers construe them to mean; and that the roles and self-concepts of the observers themselves are also constructions, created at least in part by their interpreted observations.[1]

This study is an essay in applying that epistemological principle to politics. Rather than seeing political news as an account of events to which people react, I treat political developments as creations of the publics concerned with them. Whether events are noticed and what they mean depend upon observers' situations and the language that reflects and interprets those situations. A social problem, a political enemy, or a leader is both an entity and a signifier with a range of meanings that vary in ways we can at least partly understand. Similarly, I treat people who engage in political actions as constructions in two senses. First, their actions and their language create their subjectivity, their sense of who they are. Second, people involved in politics are symbols to other observers: they stand for ideologies, values, or moral stances and they become role models, benchmarks, or symbols of threat and evil.

My focus, in short, is upon people and developments with multiple and changing meanings to one another. That perspective offers a difficult analytic challenge because entities do not remain stable while you study them and subjects and objects are continuously evolving constructions of each other. Historical evidence and psychological theory nonetheless support these assumptions. In every era and every national culture, political controversy and maneuver have hinged upon conflicting interpretations of current actions and developments: leaders are perceived as tyrannical or benevolent, wars as just or aggressive, economic policies as supports of a class or the public interest, minorities as pathological or helpful. It is precisely such differences about the referents of politically significant signs that constitute political and social history.

If political developments depended upon factual observations, false meanings would be discredited in time and a con-

---

1. Two recent books, one by an eminent philosopher and the other by an eminent psychologist, expound the conceptual framework I apply here in some detail: Nelson Goodman, *Of Mind and Other Matters* (Cambridge: Harvard University Press, 1983); Jerome Bruner, *Actual Minds, Possible Worlds* (Cambridge: Harvard University Press, 1985).

sensus upon valid ones would emerge, at least among informed and educated observers. That does not happen, even over long time periods. The characteristic of problems, leaders, and enemies that makes them political is precisely that controversy over their meanings is not resolved. Whether poverty originates in the inadequacies of its victims or in the pathologies of social institutions, whether a leader's actions are beneficial or damaging to the polity, whether a foreign, racial, religious, or ethnic group is an enemy or a desirable ally, typify the questions that persist indefinitely and remain controversial as historical issues just as they were controversial in their time. The debates over such questions constitute politics and catalyze political action. There is no politics respecting matters that evoke a consensus about the pertinent facts, their meanings, and the rational course of action.

It is just as evident that individuals' opinions on political issues change with transformations in their social situations, with cues about the probable future consequences of political actions, with information about the sources and authoritative support for policies, and with the groups with whom they identify. The meanings of the self, the other, and the social object are facets of the same transaction, changing and remaining stable as those others do. Psychological theorists as diverse as Mead, Vygotsky, Marcuse, and Festinger concur on this point with the lesson of historical observation. The radical student who becomes a conventional liberal or conservative with graduation to new jobs and new ambition, the dedicated communist who becomes a fervent anticommunist, the liberal who becomes a neoconservative, the pacifists who support war when their country is about to embark on one, are recurring examples of the principle that political self-definitions and roles reflect the conditions, constraints, and opportunities in which people find themselves: that ideology and material conditions are part of the same transaction. To understand either stability or change, it is necessary to look to the social situations people experience, anticipate, or fantasize.

The incentive to reduce ambiguity to certainty, multivalent people to egos with fixed ideologies, and the observer's predilections to the essence of rationality pervades everyday discourse and social science practice. These premises reassure observers that their own interpretations are defensible. And there is a related reason that the conventional view is appealing: its implicit

promise that rationality and information will end the uninter-
rupted record of war, poverty, cruelty and other evils that have
marked human history; that rational choice may never be
optimal, but is a central influence in decision making, policy
formation, and voting, and is likely to become a stronger one.

The alternative assumption denies a sharp break between the
past and the future; the political language that has rationalized
privileges, disadvantages, aggressions, and violence in the past is
likely to continue to do so; the phrase "rational choice" is one
more symbol in the process of rationalization rather than the path
to enlightenment. Pessimistic conclusions are disturbing but are
not reasons for rejecting the premises from which they flow. On
the contrary, any political analysis that encourages belief in a
secure, rational, and cooperative world fails the test of conformity to experience and to the record of history.

The kinds of empirical observations already mentioned and
others to be noted later support the view that interpretations of
political news construct diverse realities. Many influential social
theories of the twentieth century point to the same conclusion. In
his recent books Nelson Goodman has analyzed with impressive
rigor and clarity the process of what he calls "making worlds."
Goodman sees science, art, and other cultural forms as "ways of
worldmaking."[2] So far as politics is concerned, news reporting is
a major way as well, complementing scientific claims and works of
art. The realities people experience, then, are not the same for
every person or for all time, but rather are relative to social
situations and to the signifiers to which observers pay some
attention. The chapters that follow illustrate that premise.

But relativism is unsettling. It leaves us without a reassuring
test of what is real and of who we are; and relativist propositions
cannot be verified or falsified in the positivist sense because they
pose the Mannheim Paradox problem: observers who postulate
that the meanings of observations vary with the social situation or
with something else must take the same skeptical and tentative
position with respect to their own relativism.

Belief in the verifiability (or falsifiability) of observations, the
separability of facts from values, and the possibility of relying

2. Nelson Goodman, *Ways of Worldmaking* (Indianapolis: Hacket Publishing Co., 1978), and Bruner, *Actual Minds, Possible Worlds.*

upon deduction to establish valid generalizations is a formula for self-assurance, even for dogmatism, as well as for claims to power over others. But if those assumptions are invalid, if knowledge and meanings are in any sense relative to other knowledge and to the observer's social position, then neither precision in observation nor rigor in deductive reasoning will yield acceptable "covering laws" or generalizations. They offer an appearance of doing so as long as attention is diverted from the problematic premises; but reliance upon that conceptual framework for doing social science is rather like looking under the lamppost, where the light is good, for the quarter one dropped in a dark section of the street.

Critics of relativist positions charge that the latter make it impossible to test their own assumptions and conclusions because these conclusions are *also* relative to something else; but that claim should not be mistaken for an affirmation that relativist positions are false. The claim is only that they cannot be conclusively established as true. But the same must be said of the positivist position. There is reason for tentativeness about all forms of explanation. Relativist positions are not uniquely vulnerable with respect to verification or falsification. Reasons for support or for doubt are all mortals can hope for. Final conclusions, like final solutions, are for dogmatists.

There is a moral argument for rejecting relativism as well: the contention that it justifies any kind of behavior at all because it fails to provide an absolute ethical standard. Both logic and historical experience dispute that conclusion. A relativist posture in no way denies the need for a clear moral code; it recognizes, rather, that interpretations of actions do vary with social situations. Acceptance of that variation encourages careful examination of moral claims and tentativeness in applying them in ways that others might find objectionable or harmful; but it neither establishes nor undermines the moral code of an individual or a group.

It is moral certainty, not tentativeness, that historically has encouraged people to harm or kill others. Genocide, racial and religious persecution, and the rest of the long catalogue of political acts that have stained human history can only come from people who are sure that they are right. Only in bad novels and comic books do characters knowingly do evil and boast of it. In life, people rationalize their actions in moral terms, an observation that suggests that relativism is a buttress of the moral life because it encourages a critical and reflective stance toward others' actions and toward one's own.

Some critics contend that anyone who believes that realities are constructed and multiple must also believe that they are equally valid, but that conclusion does not follow. On the contrary, the notion of reality construction implies that some are valid and others not. There are multiple realities because people differ in their situations and their purposes. The reality an impressionist painter constructs respecting a maritime scene is not that of a sailor or that of an atomic physicist. The reality a destitute black person constructs respecting the nature of poverty has little validity for a conservative political candidate or a conservative political scientist or even for the same black when he is trying to achieve high grades in a business school. Every construction of a world is a demanding activity. It can be done well or badly and be right or wrong. To understand the multiple realities are prevalent is liberating, but such understanding in no way suggests that every construction is as good as every other.[3]

Social scientists who deny that there are many worlds cut themselves off from vital modes of observation and interpretation; but they reject their intellectual and moral obligations and their capabilities if they do not also recognize some realities as more valid than others for those who construct them and for social analysts.

Materialism, Idealism, and Indifference

Politicians, officials, journalists whose careers depend on news stories, advocates of causes, and a fair number of people who are continually concerned, shocked, entertained, or titillated by the news constitute an avid audience for the political spectacle. For them there are weekly, daily, sometimes hourly triumphs and defeats, grounds for hope and for fear, a potpourri of happenings that mark trends and aberrations, some of them historic. Political life is hyperreal: typically more portentous than personal affairs.

But most of the world's population, even most of the popula-

---

3. I discussed this position in *Political Language* (New York: Academic Press, 1978), 5–20. See also Goodman, *Ways of Worldmaking*, 17–22. For a contrary view, see William Connolly's review of *Political Language* in *American Political Science Review* 73 (September 1979): 847.

tion of the "advanced countries," has no incentive to define joy, failure, or hope in terms of public affairs. Politics and political news are remote, not often interesting, and for the most part irrelevant. This indifference of "the masses" to the enthusiasms and fears of people who thrive on public attention to political matters is the despair of the latter group. Public indifference is deplored by politicians and by right-thinking citizens. It is the target of civics courses, oratory, and television news shows and the reiterated theme of polls that discover how little political information the public has and how low politics rates among public concerns.

Actions that show resistance to political involvement are even more persuasive than surveys. Nonvoters constitute a larger political grouping in America than the adherents of any political party. Only a small proportion of the population contributes money for political purposes, engages in any other kind of political activity, or pays more than passing attention to political news.[4]

That indifference, which academic political science notices but treats as an obstacle to enlightenment or democracy, is, from another perspective, a refuge against the kind of engagement that would, if it could, keep everyone's energies taken up with activism: election campaigns, lobbying, repressing some and liberating others, wars, and all other political activities that displace living, loving, and creative work. Regimes and proponents of political causes know that it takes much coercion, propaganda, and the portrayal of issues in terms that entertain, distort, and shock to extract a public response of any kind. "The public" is mainly a black hole into which the political efforts of politicians, advocates of causes, the media, and the schools disappear with hardly a trace.[5] Its apathy, indifference, quiescence, and resistance to the consciousness industry[6] is especially impressive in an age of widespread literacy and virtually universal access to the

4. For survey data on the low level of political information among adults see Robert S. Erikson, Norman R. Luttbeg, and Kent L. Tedin, *American Public Opinion*, 2nd ed. (New York: Wiley, 1980), 19.

5. Jean Baudrillard, *In the Shadow of the Silent Majorities* (New York: Semiotext, 1983), 1–64.

6. The term comes from Hans Magnus Enzensberger, *The Consciousness Industry* (New York: Seabury Press, 1974).

media. Indifference to the enthusiasms and alarms of political activists has very likely always been a paramount political force, though only partially effective and hard to recognize because it is a nonaction. Without it, the slaughter and repression of diverse groups in the name of nationalism, morality, or rationality would certainly be even more widespread than it has been; for the claim that a political cause serves the public interest has often distorted or destroyed concern for personal wellbeing.

Recognition of the power that springs from indifference to political appeals is a precondition for understanding the effectiveness of political symbolism. Symbols, whether language or icons, that have no relevance to everyday lives, frustrations, and successes are meaningless and impotent. They are like the reactions of spectators in a museum to the icons of a culture with which they feel no empathy. In the measure that political advocates resort to appeals that do not touch the experiences of their audience, indifference is to be expected.

Symbols become that facet of experiencing the material world that gives it a specific meaning. The language, rituals, and objects to which people respond are not abstract ideas. If they matter at all, it is because they are accepted as basic to the quality of life. The term "unemployment" may evoke a yawn from an affluent person who has never feared it. It carries a more intense connotation in a depression than at other times even for workers who are always vulnerable to layoffs. A flag may be a garish piece of cloth, a reminder of the repressions and sufferings justified by appeals to patriotism, or an evocation of nostalgia for a land in which one grew up or for the stories about its history one learned as a child. A symbol always carries a range of diverse, often conflicting, meanings that are integral aspects of specific material and social situations. The material condition as experienced and the symbol as experienced stand for each other. The psychological processes by which they come to do so are doubtless subtle and complex and are certainly not fully understood. They may involve the displacement of private affect onto public objects, as Harold Lasswell suggested,[7] or a search for self-esteem[8] or a rational calculation,

7. Harold D. Lasswell, *Psychopathology and Politics* (Chicago: University of Chicago Press, 1930).

8. Paul M. Sniderman, *Personality and Democratic Politics* (Berkeley: University of California Press, 1975).

or a combination of functions. In any case the material basis for the symbol is critical. My references in this book to language or actions or objects that evoke meanings always presuppose that the "evocation" takes place only as a function of a specific material and social condition. Idealism and materialism are dichotomies as abstract concepts, but in everyday life they are facets of the same transaction. Every sign exercises its effect because of the specific context of privilege, disadvantage, frustration, aspiration, hope, and fear in which it is experienced.

The Incoherence of the Subject, the Object, and the Text

These observations about my conceptual framework foreshadow a more general point of view that grows out of the work of George Herbert Mead and Lev Vygotsky and is also explicit in the writings of the French poststructuralists, especially Michel Foucault and Jacques Derrida.

The subject cannot be regarded as the origin of coherent action, writing, or other forms of expression. As just noted, actions and interpretations hinge upon the social situation in which they begin, including the language that depicts a social situation. The language that interprets objects and actions also constitutes the subject. Political leaders, like all other subjects, act and speak as reflections of the situations they serially confront; their diversities and inconsistencies are statements of those situations, not of a persistent "self," for the kind of stability in action that transcends situations with varying political inducements has never existed. Chapter 3, on "political leadership," examines the sense in which that perspective undermines the premise, itself constructed very largely by the term "leader," that identifiable officials are originators of coherent courses of action. That chapter also explores the distortions in analysis implicit in the conventional assumptions about political leaders.[9]

---

9. The same lesson applies, of course, to the term "author." In writing this book I also am constituted by a range of disparate sources and inducements, including such contradictory ones as the poststructuralist writers who impress me now and the conventional political scientists I read as a graduate student and whose work I may have learned too well. If the idea that language that depicts discontinuity is itself discontinuous and self-contradictory induces a sense of vertigo, that is preferable to reassuring assumptions that divert analysis from an account of the discontinuities of the social world. The vertigo may stimulate criticism and insight.

It is probably less jarring to recognize that political objects and events are also discontinuous, sometimes contradictory, entities constituted by the signifiers and contexts that give them meanings, a point of view considered in some detail in chapters 2 and 4. Quite apart from the examples that emerge with every careful examination of a political object, entities are necessarily incoherent because the language that constructs their meaning is inherently discontinuous and in some sense undermines itself.[10] Affirmations bring to consciousness evidence for the contrary position, which the affirmations try to blunt, a form of inversion and sometimes of self deception that is especially pervasive in political language. When an American official claims that client states like El Salvador or Guatemala are protecting human rights, the statement also reminds those who hear it of evidence that they are not doing so. Every instance of language and action resonates with the memory, the fear, or the anticipation of other signifiers, so that there are radiating networks of meaning that vary with the situations of spectators and actors.

That framework gives political action, talk, writing, and news reporting a different import from that taken for granted in politicans' statements and in conventional social science writing. Accounts of political issues, problems, crises, threats, and leaders now become devices for creating disparate assumptions and beliefs about the social and political world rather than factual statements. The very concept of "fact" becomes irrelevant because every meaningful political object and person is an interpretation that reflects and perpetuates an ideology. Taken together, they comprise a spectacle which varies with the social situation of the spectator and serves as a meaning machine: a generator of points of view and therefore of perceptions, anxieties, aspirations, and strategies. The conventional distinction between procedures and outcomes loses its salience because both are now signifiers, generators of meanings that shape political quiescence, arousal, and support or opposition to causes. The denotations of key political terms become suspect because lead-

10. The point is developed in the work of Jacques Derrida, and also in Kenneth Burke's writing on political rhetoric. See Burke, *The Grammar of Motives* (New York: McGraw-Hill, 1945).

ers are not originators of courses of action, problems are not necessarily undesirable conditions to be solved, and enemies need not do or threaten harm. Instead, the uses of all such terms in specific situations are strategies, deliberate or unrecognized, for strengthening or undermining support for specific courses of action and for particular ideologies.

The political entities that are most influential upon public consciousness and action, then, are fetishes: creations of observers that then dominate and mystify their creators. I try here to analyze the pervasive consequences of the fetishism at the core of politics, never a wholly successful enterprise because it is tempting to exorcise a fetish by constructing a rational theory of politics.

2 The Construction and Uses of Social Problems

Problems as Ideological Constructions

Troubling conditions that persist are a paramount theme of political discourse. Children learn about social problems in school, newspapers recount successes and setbacks in coping with them, and academic and governmental studies examine their causes, nature, incidence, and consequences. But they are rarely solved, except in the sense that they are occasionally purged from common discourse or discussed in changed legal, social or political terms as though they were different problems.[1] Alternatively, conditions accepted as inevitable or unproblematic may come to be seen as problems; and damaging conditions may not be defined as political issues at all.

Poverty, unemployment, and discrimination against minorities and women are accepted as problems today, but through much of human history they were regarded as part of the natural order, while such issues as witches in league with the devil, American Catholics as agents of the Pope, and Americans of Japanese descent as potential saboteurs were once widely accepted as problems.

Problems come into discourse and therefore into existence as reinforcements of ideologies, not simply because they are there or because they are important for wellbeing. They signify who are virtuous and useful and who are dangerous or inadequate, which actions will be rewarded and which penalized. They constitute people as subjects with particular kinds of aspirations, self-concepts, and fears, and they create beliefs about the relative importance of events and objects. They are critical in determining who exercise authority and who accept it. They construct areas of immunity from concern because those areas are not seen as

---

1. Michel Foucault's historical analyses of madness, crime, and sexuality trace such changes in discourse that constitute problems. See *Madness and Civilization* (New York: Pantheon, 1965); *Discipline and Punish* (New York: Pantheon, 1977); *The History of Sexuality* (New York: Vintage, 1980). Some American examples are discussed in chapter 6, below.

problems. Like leaders and enemies, they define the contours of the social world, not in the same way for everyone, but in the light of the diverse situations from which people respond to the political spectacle.

In this chapter I analyze the construction of conditions as problems, the diverse meanings of discourses and texts about problems in the light of the situations from which they are viewed, and some political uses of problem construction. The various sections of the chapter deal with a range of meanings and consequences of social problems. They are aspects of a common transaction because they supplement and reinforce each other so as to overdetermine an ideological stance and a pattern of public policies. This examination tries to bring into the open some implications of our language and actions regarding social problems about which officials and interest groups are usually silent, a silence or obliviousness that also buttresses preferred ideologies.

Damaging Conditions That Do Not Become Problems

If social problems are constructions, it is evident that conditions that hurt people need not become problems. Segregated restaurants, hotels, schools, and toilets in the South persisted for a century and a half without becoming problems, as have countless other racist and sexist practices everywhere. The impoverishment and massacre of a high proportion of the American Indian population was not a problem while it was happening, but only became one long after it was a fait accompli.

Peter Bachrach has called such phenomena "nondecisions."[2] Sometimes they occur because powerful political groups can block consideration of practices from which those groups benefit; but that form of nondecision is typically short-lived. The longer lasting instances stem from ideological premises that are so widespread in some people's everyday language that they are not recognized as ideological at all, but accepted as the way the world is constituted. To people socialized to see Indians, women, or homosexuals as inferior, advocates of equal rights legislation are cranks; *they* may be a problem, but discrimination against disadvantaged groups is not.

2. Cf. Peter Bachrach, *The Theory Of Democratic Elitism* (Boston: Little Brown, 1967); Peter Bachrach and Morton Baratz, *Power and Poverty* (New York: Oxford University Press, 1970).

Because there is ordinarily a consensus on long-standing social practices, only a small subset of them become problems, and these are not likely to be the most damaging. Agreement on most established practices, moreover, makes general toleration of a smaller set of "problems" all the easier. Perhaps the most powerful influence of news, talk, and writing about problems is the immunity from notice and criticism they grant to damaging conditions that are not on the list. The result of this aspect of problem construction is the creation of faith in the moral sensitivity of regimes and individuals while erasing lapses that would raise questions about that sensitivity.

Problems as Benefits

A high proportion of the social problems in the news are present for long periods of time or only intermittently absent. Crime, poverty, unemployment, and discrimination against disadvantaged groups exemplify issues that have persisted as problems for long periods.

The historical failure to pursue effective remedial action stems from a pervasive contradiction. A problem to some is a benefit to others; it augments the latter group's influence. For employers, unemployment and poverty mean reduced labor costs and a docile work force, an incentive that easily coexists with personal sympathy for the unfortunate. Discrimination against women or minorities means favored treatment for men and for majorities. The term "problem" only thinly veils the sense in which deplored conditions create opportunities.

What is the political import of terms that emphasize troubles and conceal benefits? They certainly mute conflicts of interest between social groups. They also reassure victims of problems and those who sympathize with them that concern for their plight is widespread. In these subtle ways language forms help moderate the intensity of social conflict.

As already suggested, there are other ways to refer to the benefits that problems yield: a plentiful labor supply, avoidance of governmental interference in labor and product markets, a favorable business climate, incentives to ambition, a strong national defense posture. Such references erase the link between benefits and the troubling conditions with which they are associated. The language is clearly vital to political maneuver and to the construction of subjectivity.

Exposure of the general population to contradictions in their daily lives makes it easier to mask both the ineffectiveness of solutions and the benefits some groups derive from the failure. The capitalist economy in industrialized countries affords increasing comfort, a lavish output of consumer goods that provides a choice for some and a display for others, and impressive opportunities for recreation and cultural gratification, with all these developments encouraging still higher expectations for the future. At the same time there is growing anxiety about war and the survival of the species, a chronically high level of poverty and unemployment, especially among the young, women, and minorities, and rising risks of industrial illness, industrial accidents, and contamination of food, air, and water supplies. Conflicting cues about the meaning of the good life and the promise of governmental actions create ambiguity about the social world that readily transforms into ambivalence and acquiescence respecting public policy. Ambivalence does not typically yield indecisiveness. On the contrary, it provides support both for the regime and for challenges to the regime. Contradictions in experience encourage contradictions in political action.

Problems as Ambiguous Claims

A central theme of this analysis, then, is the diversity of meanings inherent in every social problem, stemming from the range of concerns of different groups, each eager to pursue courses of action and call them solutions. National security is a different problem for each of the parties concerned with it, such as the various branches of the armed forces, the General Dynamics Corporation, that firm's workers, the Women's International League for Peace and Freedom, and potential draftees. The problem becomes what it is for each group precisely because their rivals define it differently. In this sense a problem is constituted by the differences among its definitions.

Just as problems are labels for congeries of differences, so their solutions are creations of the contradictions and vacillations that advocates of different policies promote. A problem, then, is a signifier pointing to some of the following features:

1. It focuses upon a name for an undesirable condition or a threat to well-being.

2. The governmental activities such a focus rationalizes comprise a sequence of ambiguous claims and actions that change and are frequently inconsistent with one another because they are responses to different group interests. In the name of "defense" regimes increase the arms budget, support research in universities, promote "arms control" or disarmament, build weapons systems, yield to pressures from contractors against rigorous enforcement of technical specifications, provide generous retirement programs for members of the armed forces, enrich people through cost-plus contracts, support some third world regimes and overthrow others, and so on. A similar list of diverse and inconsistent actions and claims could easily be drawn up to specify the content of policies to deal with crime, poverty, education, environmental pollution, or any other problem.

3. Such a bricolage of actions and language claims sometimes ameliorates the condition and sometimes makes it worse; but some consequences of the policies pursued are always inversions of the value formally proclaimed as the goal of the activity. The escalation of armaments in rival countries typically decreases the security of both. In the name of curtailing domestic violence the judicial system puts people to death.

On occasion a "trend" signifying consistency persists for a time in the handling of a problem: a "New Deal" or a "War on Poverty," a tightening of criminal statutes and of their enforcement, a period of international détente or of the widespread repeal or enactment of capital punishment laws. But a trend is a range of actions from which an observer constructs a label. In a period of "détente" there are also some provocations and escalations of tensions. The New Deal failed to help many workers, limited the help it offered to unions, and both hurt and helped businesses in many different ways. Its policies, like all policies, were semantically created as value-laden interpretations of differences in action and in language. A "policy," then, is a set of shifting, diverse, and contradictory responses to a spectrum of political interests.

But its name is quite another phenomenon, with a different function, offering a ground for ignoring the inconsistencies to people inclined to do so. The name typically reassures, while a focus upon policy inconsistencies and differences might be disturbing. The names for policies reflect and rationalize the dominant pattern of ideologies. In doing so they heighten the sense of dynamism the political spectacle creates. They portray accomplishment, masking hesitations in action and counterproductive strategies that minimize, cancel, or reverse claims of success.

Plainly, problem construction is a complex and subtle occurrence, a facet of the concurrent formation of the self and of the social sphere, integrally linked to the endless construction and reconstruction of political causes, role structures, and moral stances.

The Construction of Reasons for Problems

Explanations for the social problems that persist are notable for the diversity of causes and of ideologies to which they point, not for their rigor, verifiability, or explanatory power. Explanations blame social institutions, social classes, those who suffer, or those who benefit. They may locate the cause of a problem in regional characteristics, nationality, ethnicity, climate, stage of historical development, personality, or a combination of several such categories. They may be concrete or abstract. They reproduce the typologies currently fashionable in other news reporting, popular discussion, and academic writing. Such diversity is as characteristic of social scientists' explanations as of popularly accepted ones. In this form of endeavor the scientific is also the political.

To evoke a problem's origin is to assign blame and praise. Blame for recurring wars and militarism depends upon whether they are seen as originating in the plans of aggressors, the authoritarian character structure of some cultures, the chance occurrence of a sequence of events with which diplomats cannot cope, the logic implicit in industrialized societies, or the will of God. Each origin reduces the issue to a particular perspective and minimizes or eliminates others. Each reflects an ideology and rationalizes a course of action.

A particular explanation of a persisting problem is likely to strike a large part of the public as correct for a fairly long period if it reflects and reinforces the dominant ideology of that era. Consider as examples the contrast in generally accepted explanations for international tensions in the decades preceding the Second World War and in those following the war or the contrast in dominant explanations of economic recession between the liberal thirties and the conservative eighties.

The "career" of an explanation of a problem manifestly hinges in part on the acceptability of the ideological premise it implies. Because a social problem is not a verifiable entity but a construction that furthers ideological interests, its explanation is bound to be part of the process of construction rather than a set of falsifiable propositions. In a crucial sense problems are created so that particular reasons can be offered for public acceptance, and, as I note below, so that particular remedies can be proposed.

An explanation for a chronic social problem can never be generally supported. It is offered to be rejected as much as to be accepted. Its function is to intensify polarization and so maintain the support of advocates on both sides. The reasons offered are crucial to the self esteem of concerned people and to the viability of interested groups, organizations, and causes. They all draw support from the evocation of a spectacle that shows their rivals as threats. An explanation for a troubling condition is typically more important to partisans than the possibility of eliminating the condition; the latter is a rhetorical evocation of a remote future time unlikely to arrive, while the explanation is vital to contemporary political maneuver.

Because there are always conflicting explanations, any affirmation of an origin for a problem is also an implicit rejection of alternative origins; such an affirmation is bound to bring to consciousness whatever it denies. As Derrida notes, the trace of what is negated remains present and so continues to play a part in action and in attitudes, its difference from the affirmation actually constructing the meaning of the affirmation. To declare that a Russian proposal for mutual reductions in armaments is only a public relations ploy is to arouse the suspicion that it may be more than that.

Oppositions in expressed "opinion" accordingly make for social stability; they are almost synonymous with it, for they reaffirm and reify what everyone already knows and accepts. To express a pro-choice or an anti-abortion position is to affirm that the opposite position is being expressed as well and to accept the opposition as a continuing feature of public discourse. The well-established, thoroughly anticipated, and therefore ritualistic reaffirmation of the differences institutionalizes both rhetorics, minimizing the chance of major shifts and leaving the regime wide discretion, for there will be anticipated support and opposition no matter what forms of action or inaction occur. As long as there is substantial expression of opinion on both sides of an issue, social stability persists and so does regime discretion regardless of the exact numbers or of marginal shifts in the numbers. The persistence of unresolved problems with conflicting meanings is vital.

It is not the expression of opposition but of consensus that makes for instability. When statements need not be defended against counterstatements, they are readily changed or inverted. Consensual agreements about the foreign enemy or ally yield readily to acceptance of the erstwhile enemy as ally and the former ally as enemy, as happened at the end of World War II; but opinions about abortion are likely to persist.[3] Rebellion and revolution do not ferment in societies in which there has been a long history of the ritualized exchange of opposing views on issues accepted as important, but rather where such exchanges have been lacking, so that a consensus on common action to oust the regime is easily built.

These observations seem counterintuitive only when opinion is conceptualized as growing in the individual mind, which then secretes it into the public domain. As soon as "opinion" is recognized as an ambiguous reference to texts, as bits of language that circulate in a culture and present themselves for acceptance or rejection, it becomes evident that opposing texts become bulwarks of one another while isolated texts, unsupported by opposition, are readily vulnerable to new language.

Language about origins is therefore not likely to convert people from an ideology to a contrary one very often or generate an opinion that persists in spite of exposure to changing language or new situations. Its effect, as already suggested, is to sharpen the issue, sometimes to polarize opinion, and in any case to clarify the pattern of opinion oppositions available for acceptance. The construction of problems and of reasons for them accordingly

---

3. For an insightful discussion of this point, see Jean Baudrillard, *Simulations* (New York: Semotext, 1983), 131–38. I treated it as well in *Politics As Symbolic Action* (New York: Academic Press, 1977), 46–47.

reinforces conventional social cleavages: those long standing divisions of interest in which relative power, sanctions, and the limits of the rivalry are well established and widely recognized. The political result of such reinforcement is clear enough. Realignments, new coalitions, and unconventional forms of political action are excluded from common discourse and so become less likely. The evocation and reconstruction of origins are pervasive, constant, and central to political maneuver, a linguistically generated process that creates concerned groups, pits them against one another for varying time periods, and gives the political process an appearance of dynamism and tension that rarely has any bearing upon its outcomes.

The Constitution of Authorities

The language that constructs a problem and provides an origin for it is also a rationale for vesting authority in people who claim some kind of competence. Willingness to suspend one's own critical judgment in favor of someone regarded as able to cope creates authority.[4] If poverty stems from individual inadequacies, then psychologists, social workers, and educators have a claim to authority in dealing with it; but if an economy that fails to provide enough jobs paying an adequate wage is the source of poverty, then economists have a claim to authority. Military threats, crime, mental illness, illiteracy, and every other problem yield claims to authority, though the claim is disputed in each case because diverse reasons for the problem compete for acceptance.

People with credentials accordingly have a vested interest in specific problems and in specific origins for them. A high proportion of political conflicts involve the advancement of such claims: foreign aggression versus American militarism as the problem; coddling criminals versus poverty; human rights violations and despotism in a third world country versus Russian support for rebels. The definition of the problem generates authority, status, profits, and financial support while denying these benefits to competing claimants. It is hardly surprising, then, that virtually all political communication directly or implicitly constructs particular problems as crucial while denigrating others.

4. Cf. Herbert A. Simon, *Administrative Behavior* (New York: Macmillan, 1947), Chap. 9.

Occasionally a problem so extensively captures attention that many claimants to authority compete to become identified with it. The Russian threat is doubtless the paramount twentieth century example, with scientists, educators, politicians, security experts and many types of administrative officials offering their services to deal with it. In the middle 1980s child abuse was constituted as an urgent problem with the result that psychologists, police officials, teachers, physicians, and neighbors all found that it could help bolster their authority, and district attorneys tried to build political careers on the prosecution of alleged abusers.

Why do some problems become "fashionable" in this way while others that are equally or more damaging never do? Why is homelessness not the kind of problem with which a range of authorities compete to become identified? It seems plausible that the difference lies in their implications for whose power is augmented and whose threatened. Child abuse, like drug abuse and the Soviet threat, offers opportunities for controlling the behaviors and the language of large numbers of people who wield little power and may be suspect on other grounds; a focus on the problem reinforces established inequalities. A serious effort to deal with homelessness, by contrast, would entail a reexamination of established economic and social institutions and so might threaten existing power inequalities.

Some efforts to secure benefits through an emphasis on a troubling problem are cynical, but most are doubtless sincere. Motivation is not the point, but rather the integral link between claims about problems and value allocations through politics. In this form of construction it is obvious that language and material benefits are part of the same transaction.

The Construction of Problems to Justify Solutions

Most academic writing accepts the same view of the link between social problems and attempts to solve them as public officials like to espouse: that as problems appear, responsible agencies search for the best way to cope with them; or, in the qualification suggested by Herbert Simon, they search for a solution that is satisfactory. The emphasis is on the rationality of the search process even if it is bounded.

But the striking characteristic of the link between political problems and solutions in everyday life is that the solution typically comes first, chronologically and psychologically. Those who favor a particular course of governmental action are likely to cast about for a widely feared problem to which to attach it in order to maximize its support.[5] This process is not necessarily self-conscious or deliberately deceptive. Those who recognize that the attachment of a favored course of action to a problem will get them what they want can easily persuade themselves of the rationality and morality of their rhetorical appeals as part of the process of persuading others. Discussions of problems arouse, widen, and deepen public interest by appealing to ideological or moral concerns, as already noted. In this sense the name for a problem is a condensation symbol, just as the name for a political goal is a condensation symbol.[6] Goals are carrots and problems are sticks; both are inducements to support measures people might otherwise find painful, unwise, or irrelevant to their lives.

Those who favor tax reductions for the rich, or for the poor, are likely to espouse the cuts regardless of the state of the economy or the current tax structure and to see their proposal as helpful in curbing inflation, unemployment, recession, or any other economic problem currently in the news. The link between problems and preferred solutions is itself a construction that transforms an ideological preference into a rational governmental action. When the MX missile proposal was losing political support in the early 1980s because the missile silos were shown to be vulnerable to attack, President Ronald Reagan and other proponents of the missiles began to portray them as the solution to a different problem: that of enhancing national bargaining power in armaments negotiations. The MX became a "bargaining chip" now that it was unimpressive as a weapon. Because the two problems appealed to different groups of people, proponents of the MX continued over the next several years to depict it as the solution to both these problems. The attachment of a solution to a problem that

5. This conclusion is somewhat similar to the premise of the "garbage can theory" of administrative decision making suggested by James March and Johan Olsen in their *Ambiguity and Choice in Organization* (Bergen, Norway: Universitetsforlaget, 1976).

6. See chapter 6, below.

occasions wide concern couches discourse in rational form; the form is critical in winning public support.

Actions justified as solutions to a problem of wide concern often bring consequences that are controversial. Michel Foucault made the point with his usual acumen in an analysis of the consequences of what is labeled a "penalty," a solution to the commission of a crime:

Penalty would . . . appear to be a way . . . of laying limits of tolerance, of giving free reign to some, of putting pressure on others, of
excluding a particular section, of making another useful, of neutralizing
certain individuals and of profiting from others. In short, penalty does
not simply "check" illegalities; it differentiates them, it provides them
with a general "economy" and, if one can speak of justice, it is not only
because the law itself in the way of applying it served the interest of a
class, it is also because the differential administration of illegalities
through the mediation of penalty forms part of those mechanisms of
domination.[7]

Foucault's point holds for solutions to some other problems as well. Therapy is help to the emotionally distressed, but it is also a signal of the limits of tolerance, a device for exerting pressure on some and giving authority to others, for differentiating, and for serving a class interest. Welfare benefits and unemployment compensation manifestly serve the same range of functions. Security checks and internal intelligence activities, "solutions" to the problem of subversion, do so in a more blatant way.

Not surprisingly, conflicting claims about which problem an action helps solve are endemic to politics, for the connection of a policy that benefits a specific group to a problem of broader concern widens support for the policy. Those who stand to gain financially or ideologically from a military contract see it, and depict it, as a contribution to national security. Medicaid does not win political support because it enriches affluent physicians but because it aids the poor. Any analysis of policy formation that accepts the wider issue as "the reason" for the action (as rational choice theories typically do) romanticizes the grounds for governmental action and so incorrectly predicts which policies will find organized and intense advocates.

7. Foucault, *Discipline and Punish*, 7.

The Construction of Gestures as Solutions

There are always people who benefit, or think they do, from a widespread belief that a problem has been solved or that there has been substantial progress toward its solution. When the number of such people is large or they occupy strategic positions, a regime has a strong incentive to depict as a solution any development that is associated with the problem linguistically, logically, or in fantasy.

The most common course is the enactment of a law that promises to solve or ameliorate the problem even if there is little likelihood it will accomplish its purpose. Though this device is rather widely recognized,[8] it is perennially effective in achieving quiescence from the discontented and legitimation for the regime. Regulatory statutes that leave consumers vulnerable to economic power, disarmament treaties that permit or foster arms buildups, welfare actions that do little to help the distressed, and anticrime laws that have little impact upon the frequency or incidence of crime remain politically useful. The Reagan administration was successful in 1984 in focusing attention on a small decline in unemployment from the high levels it had reached in the President's first administration rather than on its absolute level, which remained higher than it had been when Reagan was inaugurated.

In some policy areas the focus upon an event that promises more than it delivers has become ritualized. In international diplomacy the publicized release of some prisoners is repeatedly depicted as a signal of progress toward guaranteeing human rights, even if torture, murder, or imprisonment of political opponents continues. The conspicuous scheduling of an election in a third world country known for its despotic rule is accepted as evidence of a turn toward democracy. Political maneuver thrives upon publicized actions that mean less than meets the eye. A

8. Some studies that examine gestures as solutions in this sense are: Thurman Arnold, *The Folklore of Capitalism* (New Haven: Yale University Press, 1937); Avery Leiserson, *Administrative Regulation* (Chicago: University of Chicago Press, 1942); Marver Bernstein, *Regulating Business by Independent Commission* (Princeton: Princeton University Press, 1955); Murray Edelman, *The Symbolic Uses of Politics* (Urbana: University of Illinois Press, 1964).

closely related gesture entails the presentation of a development that benefits a particular group as one that serves everyone. The tax reductions of 1981 and 1982 were major benefits to the very wealthy and token gestures to the poor but were generally described and accepted simply as a "tax cut."

The disposition to accept official interpretations of publicized actions about matters remote from daily experience is a major source of legitimation. That disposition is understandable as a response to the pervasive ambiguity of governmental actions. Their motivations, their consequences, and the problems to which they are attached are typically unclear and the focus of controversy. For a public anxious to understand them or only marginally interested, an official cue readily becomes the key influence.

The lesson of this pervasive phenomenon is that in politics there can be no conclusive test of the logical or empirical relevance of language or other actions. A verbal or physical gesture that takes the *form* of a response to a problem frees concerned groups to bargain in line with their resources: money, tactical skills, public sympathy, and bilateral or multilateral accommodations with one another. Ambiguous language is a sign and a facilitator of bargaining.

The Perpetuation of Problems through Policies to Ameliorate Them

As noted earlier, attacks on troubling conditions are often half-hearted, inconsistent, and ineffective because of conflicting material and ideological interests. The construction of problems sometimes carries with it a more farreaching perverse effect: it helps perpetuate or intensify the conditions that are defined as the problem, an outcome that typically stems from efforts to cope with a condition by changing the consciousness or the behavior of individuals while preserving the institutions that generate consciousness and behavior.

Imprisonment may help perpetuate crime by exposing prisoners to knowledgeable criminals who teach them techniques. It also eventually releases most prisoners into a society from which they have become even more estranged than they were before their imprisonment and in which they lack resources to cope in any way other than renewed resort to crime. Similarly, the regulatory remedy for business practices that exploit consumers has overlooked the systematic capacity of established political and economic organizations to reproduce their own values in institutions such as regulatory agencies.

The study of antidiscrimination laws furnishes an explanation of the counterproductive effects of many efforts to solve social problems. Legislation declaring it illegal to discriminate against people because of their race or their sex may deter some offenses, and there are occasional prosecutions; but it is hard to say whether such laws have had a significant impact upon discrimination, even in the rare cases in which they have been enforced resolutely. Sophisticated research on this issue concludes that regardless of the formal actions it occasionally generates, this form of legislation reaffirms the very differences in dignity and treatment it is intended to eradicate. The law defines the people it ostensibly helps as victims in need of protection. This sign of their debased status legitimizes the view that is already widespread, adding to the ideological pressures against effective enforcement of the laws. More important, it contributes to a low sense of self-worth in victims of discrimination and to the public impression of them as inferior. In lengthy interviews with people who had suffered from discrimination, Kristin Bumiller found that they had internalized this view, so that, in most instances, people who had suffered discrimination chose not to pursue their legal remedies, convinced that it was not worth the trouble or that they deserved what they got. The enactment of antidiscrimination statutes salves liberals' consciences but also helps make discriminatory actions acceptable. Bumiller concludes that antidiscrimination law becomes part of the process of victimization.[9] Her sensitive analysis flouts liberal and conservative ideology, but it offers an explanation that is applicable to other governmental remedies for social problems as well. Legal language and directives to administrative agencies to correct inequities reassure people who worry about fairness, especially those who do not themselves suffer from bias. In performing this function they make it politically and morally possible to acquiesce in prejudicial

9. Kristin Bumiller, "Victims in the Shadow of the Law: A Critique of the Model of Legal Protection," *Signs* 12 (1987): 421–31; Kristin Bumiller, *The Civil Rights Society: The Social Construction of Victims* (Baltimore: Johns Hopkins University Press, 1988).

practices, the more so because the laws help induce victims of discrimination to accept their lot.

Proposals to solve chronic social dilemmas by changing the attitudes and the behavior of individuals are expressions of the same power structure that created the problems itself. In publicizing remedies that fail to alter the structure these proposals help win public acquiescence in its continuation. Labels like "remedy" and their accompanying actions become buttresses of the problems they purport to solve.

Problems as Negations of Other Problems

The emergence of any problem may divert public attention from a different one that can be more threatening. Such covert masking of more ominous conditions is a property of discourse about public issues and often an explanation for the willingness of a large public to accept an issue as legitimate even if they have no particular interest in remedying it. That attention to a conspicuous problem may reduce interest in a more troubling one is sometimes consciously recognized but more often subconsciously sensed.

While sympathy for the poor animates many people who support antipoverty measures, for example, some liberals and many conservatives doubtless find poverty a palatable problem, at least in part, because concern with that issue makes it easier to avoid attention to inequalities. Both the New Deal of the thirties and the War on Poverty of the sixties did a great deal to alleviate poverty for a time, but neither lessened inequality, and they may have increased it.[10] Antipoverty programs cost money; but measures to lessen inequality threaten established institutions, authority, and privileges. The focus upon poverty permits people to sympathize with the poor while averting a threat to the basic institutions of the polity and the economy.

In the same way the appeal of an emphasis upon the pathologies of criminals and the utility of punishing them lies partly in what it negates: the tracing of crime to pathological social conditions. This observation applies as well to other problems

10. Cf. Robert D. Plotnick and Felicity Skidmore, *Progress Against Poverty* (New York: Academic Press, 1975), 104–5, 169–79.

that focus upon individual deviance: worker and student absenteeism, rioting, rebellion, divorce, mental illness.

Discourse about social problems and their political management carries meaning concurrently on several levels. It is manifestly a dialogue about some named conditions and about appropriate courses of action; but the same discourse can be a latent statement about more troubling matters. To put the point another way, silence is meaningful when it represents avoidance of an issue that is divisive if mentioned. The strategic function of political language is apparent in such instances.

There is also a competition for attention among the problems that are publicly discussed. As some come to dominate political news and discussion, others fade from the scene. There seems to be a limit upon the number of issues people notice and worry about regardless of their severity. Anthony Downs has written about "issue-attention cycles"; after a time an issue begins to bore the public and is replaced with something else even if it has not been resolved.[11] Ghetto riots were headline news from the 1964 Watts riot until about 1967 and then were reduced to minor items, even though the ghettos continued to erupt in violent protest through at least the early seventies.[12] The logic that explains official, public, and media attention to political problems does not turn on their severity but rather upon their dramatic appeals. These, in turn, are vulnerable to satiation of attention and to novelty.

Perhaps the most frequent application of this principle lies in the capacity of foreign threats to diminish attention to domestic conditions. Leaders have often maintained a supportive following by focusing attention on foreign threats that divert concern from unsolved domestic troubles. While each domestic problem typically hurts only a small proportion of the population, there are always foreign problems that can credibly be presented as pressing threats to everyone. Rebellion in a small third world country becomes a domino that will topple more important

11. Anthony Downs, "Up and Down with Ecology: The Issue-Attention Cycle," *The Public Interest,* no. 28 (Summer, 1972): 38–50.
12. Cf. Michael Lipsky and David J. Olson, *Commission Politics: The Processing of Racial Crisis in America* (New Brunswick: Transaction Books, 1977), 446–47.

countries. National security is a key symbol because fear of foreign attack is a contagion that spreads widely and rapidly.

The news, then, conveys some covert information about the set of problems of which the public is aware, even when it purports to deal with a specific issue. The world people experience as the wider setting for their everyday lives is a chameleon world that transforms its contours with the changing cues that news accounts convey: the context of public knowledge and of problems that compete for attention. To ask people to react to the name of a problem in a survey therefore may have little bearing on their reactions as they go about their daily affairs. The very mention of a problem evokes a reaction, so that its prominence or its absence in the media or in other situations is a key element which a survey inevitably distorts. A change to a socialist government in Grenada was hardly perceived as a problem or even prominently reported until a subsequent American invasion of the island retroactively gave that governmental change an ominous significance. The single problem takes its meaning from the constellation of problems with which it overlaps and from narratives about its past and its future consequences.

The past, the present, and the future are all transformed as new problems seize attention. After defeat in Vietnam, past military ventures became suspect for a time and future ones even more so; and after Reagan's election, a part of the public repudiated these suspicions of military strategies and reinvented a future in which military might guarantees peace. The past and the future people construct are bound to be rationalizations of their current social worlds and of the public policies to which they subscribe.

News accounts therefore reconstruct social worlds, histories, and eschatologies, evoking grounds for concern and for hope and assumptions about what should be noticed and what ignored, who are respectable or heroic, and who not respectable. News items displace others and in turn take their meaning from other accounts, always in the context of a perspective about history and ideology. Little wonder, then, that interest groups try to shape the content and the form of television and printed news, for to create a world dominated by a particular set of problems is at the same time to create support for specific courses of action.

The Uses of Invisible Social Problems

The evidence for some social problems is the experience of their victims, while others become known only from the claims of people with an interest in publicizing them. High unemployment, toxic materials in the air or water, assaults in the city streets, and foreign invasions are examples of conditions that their victims experience in their everyday lives. Each such problem creates some support for measures to counter it. Although there is always controversy about how severe the condition is, what caused it, and what should be done about it, information comes from a wide range of credible sources.

The case is different for warnings about the hostile intentions of domestic or foreign regimes, charges that welfare checks destroy character, or allegations that fetuses feel pain as they are aborted. Such claims cannot find confirmation in anyone's experience; but they win support for policies nonetheless. They are typically more effective in attracting political support than the problems that can be examined, for those who find such claims ideologically appealing need not worry about counterevidence. Few are likely to deny that a recession or industrial accidents are problems even if they are unaffected themselves, for it is apparent that such conditions can be documented. The absence of controversy about their existence leaves room for disinterest, apathy, or only intermittent attention to them. To the advocate of strong measures to counter subversive activities, by contrast, apathy becomes evidence of softness toward enemies; moral passion is inflamed against people who deny that the problem exists or refuse to see it as threatening.

A central function of some public administrative agencies is the publicizing of narratives about threats remote from daily experience, for these narratives create the rationale for intelligence organizations, national police agencies, and departments of defense. Groups that benefit from public concern about such threats provide an active constituency for these organizations. They focus on an otherwise amorphous, diffuse set of interests and afford them an enhanced opportunity for influence both through their recounting of stories and through the spectacle of dramatic action they create to cope with enemies who are ordinarily unseen.

The Definition of Events as Crises

The terms "problem" and "crisis" are inducements to acquiesce in deprivations. For most people they awaken expectations that *others* will tolerate deprivations. "Problem" connotes a condition that is resistant to facile solution because it stems from entrenched institutional features or entrenched character flaws. Those who are untouched by it, those who benefit from it, and those who suffer from it all learn that it is likely to continue. A "crisis," by contrast, heralds instability; it usually means that people must endure new forms of deprivation for a time. In the conventional view, then, problems are chronic (though curable in principle) and crises are acute; but the distinction turns out to be arbitrary when the catalysts of crises are examined.[13]

More often than not a crisis is an episode in a long sequence of similar problems. No characteristic of any episode makes it the precipitant of a crisis; it is apparently possible to elevate any incident to that role. Troop movements in a potentially hostile country that are ignored or explained away as routine on some occasions become evidence at other times that a war crisis has developed. In 1974 signs that swine flu might become widespread the next winter were treated as heralding a health crisis, justifying alarmist warnings and forced innoculations that themselves killed many people, though similar signs and a higher incidence of flu in other years are treated as routine. The positioning of Russian missiles in Cuba in 1962 precipitated a "Cuban Missile Crisis" though the stationing of American missiles as close to the Soviet Union even earlier was not defined as a crisis by either country. A crisis, like all news developments, is a creation of the language used to depict it; the appearance of a crisis is a political act, not a recognition of a fact or of a rare situation.

Like "problems," crises typically rationalize policies that are

13. I discuss some other connotations of the term "crisis" in my *Political Language* (New York: Academic Press, 1977), 43–49.

especially harmful to those who are already disadvantaged. Wars, recessions, depressions, severe earthquakes, and steep price rises impose especially heavy burdens on the poor and the powerless, while they also justify increases in the power of regimes. The class-based result of crisis labeling is unintended. It does not stem from plotting but from a skewed structure of opportunities and protections and from ideology inherent in language interpretation that reinforces that skewed structure.

Audiences as Creators of Social Problems

Whether a condition is a social problem hinges, by definition, on whether a sizeable part of the public accepts it as one. But more than tautology is involved for it is audience acceptance that makes it possible for interest groups, public officials, or anyone else to portray a set of conditions as a problem, just as obliviousness to conditions that are ruinous to many people prevents their labeling as problems.

Public attention to troublesome but remote conditions is likely to be ephemeral, changing forms as the news highlights different issues or unrecognized facets of old ones. An equally striking characteristic of public attention lies in its capacity to be both present and absent: to be selective in the occasions it manifests its existence. Those who assume they cannot influence a condition do not clamor for governmental action to change it, no matter how serious it may be for them. The condition then seems to be regarded as fated: an inevitable feature of the universe, therefore not a problem to be resolved. Urban decay, structural unemployment, inadequate intercity transportation, farm surpluses, and many other noxious social conditions have come to be accepted as unpleasant aspects of the contemporary world over which people have little or no control. While they are present as abstract problems and as physical phenomena, they are absent as pressing political issues and remain unnoticed by much of the population much of the time. The accepted modes of reference to them deplore them as nuisances or as evils while avoiding proposals to use resources to eliminate them. It is largely problems that are damaging to the groups with few resources for influence that are treated as fated, uncontrollable, or invisible.

In a rather similar way warnings that a course of action will occasion severe future problems are easily ignored so long as such claims rest upon premises that are not readily understood or are ideologically unpalatable. They may even be believed but remain in a different universe of discourse from discussions of ameliorative action; Watergate in the 1972 election campaign and high deficits in the 1984 campaign are examples.

Unless their audience is receptive to the depiction of a condition as a problem, leaders and interest groups cannot use it to their advantage. Interpretations are likely to be diverse and they are often unstable or ambivalent. At some level of consciousness people doubtless sense that they wield this kind of power to acquiesce in elite definitions of problems or to nullify them by ignoring them. The obliviousness of "the masses" to a high proportion of the issues that seize the attention of those with an avid interest in public affairs is a potent political weapon for most of the people of the world though it remains largely unrecognized in academic writing.[14] "The news" is made, reported, interpreted, and read by a small fraction of the population, some of whom it preoccupies; and it is ignored, resisted, or only intermittently noticed by the overwhelming majority. The evidences of general political apathy and quiescence in the face of determined and continuous efforts to awaken interest in "public affairs" are persuasive: widespread ignorance of the information that is most often publicized and stressed in news reports and in early schooling; the inconsistency of many beliefs about "important" political issues; a high incidence of nonvoting.

Political activists and public officials find obliviousness to their causes frustrating when, as is often the case, the actions they favor entail sacrifice or suffering for the apathetic population. That is the consequence of military actions, tax increases, and other policies that bring material or moral deprivations. Advocates of such policies see the costs as necessary to cope with problems, so they try to impress upon the nonactivists that sacrifice is warranted, even noble, an enterprise that is difficult if their potential audiences are not paying attention. Advocates of these policies succeed on occasion; but they know that they would be successful more often if their audiences were as politicized as they.

It is not surprising, then, that there are constant efforts to

14. *Cf.* Jean Baudrillard, *In the Shadow of the Silent Majorities* (New York: Semiotext, 1983), pp. 1–64.

bring such politicization about: polemics about the duty and efficacy of voting; dramatically presented news stories that emphasize alleged threats to personal well-being and the public interest; reliance upon politicians and interest group spokespersons who are persuasive "communicators"; resort to the contriving of dramatic events ("pseudoevents") in order to win media publicity. The politicized minority assumes that its target public needs alarms, shocks, and titillation to make it pay attention to the issues that preoccupy that minority. They assume as well that these devices need to be supplemented with a measure of coercion to win acquiescence in the more severe forms of sacrifice "in the public interest." Policies that can be implemented without immediate public acquiescence and whose later consequences are not easily traced to the actions that initiated them are exceptions. Monetary policy, for example, involves technical controls over money supply and interest rates that receive little publicity, while their ultimate consequences in unemployment or higher prices appear to be the fault of market forces against which there is no recourse.

Whether the many people who pay little or no attention to most news accounts thereby damage or enhance their well-being depends upon what we assume news accounts do. In the conventional view, they provide information that enables people to act in their own interests. In the view generally accepted by students of discourse and of political language, they construct the social reality to which people respond and help construct the subjectivity of actors and spectators as well; in the process, they reinforce established power structures and value hierarchies. The second perspective therefore suggests that preoccupation with the news is more nearly a form of subjugation than an aid to autonomy. People are not helpless before the influence of news makers and media; but there is constant straining to maintain detachment and autonomy.

The Devaluation of Everyday Experience

Even when it can be confirmed, news of public affairs consists largely of stories about events remote from everyday life: statements by public officials and other names that are familiar only through their constant appearance in the media; troop movements and natural disasters in distant places; crimes by and against people one does not know; statements about "trends": in opinion, prices, population movements, welfare rolls; predictions of the future by people one does not know. To hear or read the news is to live intermittently in a world one does not touch in daily life; and not to read it ordinarily makes little difference, with the important exception that the mind does not then focus on the realities news stories construct.

Most experiences that make life joyful, poignant, boring, or worrisome are not part of the news: the grounds for personal concern, frustration, encouragement and hope; the conditions that matter at work, at home, and with friends; the events people touch, as distinct from those that are "reported"; the experience of financial distress or of opulence; children in trouble; lovers; alienating or gratifying jobs.

On occasion news reports and personal experiences converge. The unemployed woman who witnesses a television portrayal of long lines of applicants for unemployment insurance benefits sees her worry mirrored in the lives of others. That example helps us understand how the media and everyday life interact and also in what ways they remain insulated from each other. News about "public affairs" encourages the translation of personal concerns into beliefs about a public world people witness as spectators rather than as participants. The quality of daily life and of personal well-being becomes a private affair, divorced from the realm of public affairs, which is constructed as the sphere that really matters so far as governmental policy is concerned. Everyone is taught that influence should be exerted in the public realm even though the news reports from that world also imbue the public with the view that stronger and more fundamental forces than their own wishes are critical: economic conditions, military imbalances, majority votes, psychological needs and impulses, and other constructs that teach people how impotent they are against complex, remote, and untouchable developments. In this sense the news helps everyone to accept their experienced lives by creating another world of symbols and fetishes. The political spectacle encourages people to support good causes and leaders and to oppose enemies, to sacrifice for the common welfare and to acquiesce in the inevitable. In doing so it encourages acceptance of the stable social structures and the inequalities that shape their experiences.

Here we touch on a central consequence of the construction of public problems. It denigrates the concerns of everyday existence and personal well-being so as to highlight the constructions that originate in reports about the political spectacle. These change often. They call attention to the long odds against success in changing social conditions and to the irrelevance of personal sensibility. Though the spectacle takes place in a remote universe, it discourages resistance to immanent conditions and it rationalizes acceptance of the world as it is.

Social Problems as Texts:
Proliferation, Erasure, Traces, Supplements

These various constructions and uses of social problems typically act together rather than as single influences. They evoke each other, or they complement, rationalize, displace, or qualify one other. A problem constructed to justify a course of action, for example, gives rise to an explanation that rationalizes still other policies. Gestures that have little impact upon the problem they purport to solve may occasion new policies that get attached to a different problem. Problems that are displaced by more dramatic ones reappear in changed circumstances, calling for new explanations, new gestures, and perhaps still other displacements, negations, or a crisis, even while the proliferating spectacle devalues everyday experience.

In short, each action or term carries the trace of others, constructing an exploding set of scenes and signs that move in unpredictable directions and that radiate endlessly, actions and the language that defines their meaning evoking still other acts and terms that are supplementary, contradictory, or logically irrelevant.

The construction of problems, then, is as much a way of knowing and a way of acting strategically as a form of description; and it is often a way of excluding systematic attention to history and to social structure as well. The challenge, for those who act and for those who try to understand, is to recognize the range of meanings and of strategies implicit in each item that emerges from the radiation of signifiers. As the political spectacle sequentially arouses, reassures, interests, or bores diverse groups of people, it constructs them as agents of one or another social course, even while they play their parts in reconstruction of the spectacle.

3 The Construction and Uses of Political Leaders

Political leaders become signs of competence, evil, nationalism, future promise, and other virtues and vices and so help introduce meaning to a confusing political world. In assigning meanings to leaders, spectators define their own political postures. At the same time belief in leadership is a catalyst of conformity and obedience. A term that excites the imaginations of large numbers of people and also helps to organize and discipline them is a potent political instrument, though an uncertain one in its consequences.

Leaders are controversial in their own time and they remain so as historical figures, though their meanings change as discourses and preoccupations do. In the late twentieth century some saw Lincoln as a racist rather than a Great Emancipator, a savior of the union, or an oppressor of the South. Henry Kissinger's performance as Secretary of State made his model, Metternich, controversial again: the genius at resolving international controversy or the preserver of old oligarchies against ferment for change.

Whatever its current connotation, talk about a leader is an ideological text. Like all terms that appear often in discussions of politics, "leadership" introduces diverse language games that vary with the social context. References to leaders of one's own country, interest groups, friendly or hostile foreign countries, bureaucratic organizations, riots, or revolutions initiate disparate chains of associations that vary with the current situations of observers and are often multifaceted and contradictory. In each case the leader personifies a range of fears and hopes. As a sign, "leadership" combines wide ambiguity and strong affect.

But these political uses are different from the connotations that generate the term's continuing popular appeal. The latter entail systematic contradictions. The central connotation of "leadership" is innovation: leaders point the way so that others can emulate their initiatives. Yet we also know that political leaders must follow their followers, that conformity to widely held ideology is typically the key to success in winning and retaining high office and that originality is risky. History and theory suggest that followers create leaders rather than the converse.

A related support for leadership lies in the assumption that political leaders cope with the dilemmas and the threats to their security that most citizens fear. Yet "strong" leaders typically win their reputations through policies that bring risk, suffering, or death to large numbers of people. If yearning for security and protection creates leaders, leaders themselves do more than their share to construct the threats to well-being that keep those aspirations alive.

Linked to these contradictions is the inclination of fervent supporters of political leaders to place them above the political battle and the consequent efforts of aspirants to high office to create the same impression. Implicit in the notion of an exalted office above mundane politics is an ability to know what is best for the public and what policies will ward off dangers. But analysis and intellectual guidance are typically functions of staff members and bureaus, not of leaders. The latter may take their advice, but only when it is politic to do so.

As a signifier, then, leadership connotes innovation, but leaders emerge and maintain their positions only when they embrace current fashions and beliefs. That contradiction illuminates the utility of the term and the phenomenon. Leaders win acclaim and their followers win reassurance and hope from courses of action that reaffirm accepted ideologies while connoting boldness, intelligence, change, and paternal protection. The deprivations and powerlessness that characterize the lives of most citizens furnish the incentive to believe in leaders who signify hope and a talent for coping with complex forces. In an age of mass education and mass communication the links among ambiguity in language, support for leaders, and the preservation of established differences in resources and dignity become potent.

Contradiction and murkiness about the role of powerful people are instruments of political influence because they make it easy to generate reasons to accept authority. Aspirants must create an impression that they deserve to be followed, and common mystifications help them do so. Regimes, educational institutions, and everyday rhetoric disseminate a familiar set of beliefs that serve that purpose: some people are born leaders; leaders possess certain traits (resourcefulness, originality, courage, foresight, mediating talents, self-sacrifice in the public interest) in greater degree than others; that individuals become leaders is itself evidence that they surpass others in the necessary qualities or that they represent the public will, divine will, merit, the average citizen, or whatever other symbol is accepted as legitimate at a particular time and place. To list these common-place assumptions about leadership is to raise questions about their validity; but in everyday discourse they are likely to be intoned rather than examined because leadership provides vital psychological gratifications.

The Psychological Uses of Leadership

The idea of leadership makes a complex and largely unknowable social world understandable even while it assuages personal guilt and anxiety by transferring responsibility to another. If the subtle effects of economic conjunctures, historical change, and ideologies daunt the general public as well as historians and social scientists, belief in the beneficent or malevolent power of leaders offers a satisfying resolution. If both the privileged and the disadvantaged need to exorcise their concerns about inequalities, the policies of leaders who pursue "the public interest" or obstruct it provide a gratifying explanation. Leaders are ready symbols of good or evil, while historical trends, social conditions, relations of production, and modes of discourse are not. Leaders become objectifications of whatever worries or pleases observers of the political scene because it is easy to identify with them, support or oppose them, love or hate them.

These sources of affect complement others. People who feel burdened by the responsibility for making difficult choices about their own lives and the lives of others can transfer that onus to a leader, can "escape from freedom" in Erich Fromm's evocative phrase. The history of the twentieth century offers abundant evidence that that incentive can be powerful in an age of mass society, formal freedoms, and sometimes disastrous economic pressures. The idea of a leader apparently offers the security and also the sternness associated with the father. These benefits of leadership usually mask the power every population enjoys to ignore leaders and their warnings about constructed threats, problems, and enemies and so deprive them of their power to impose sacrifices.

But for followers leadership also entails fear of hostility from the powerful and anxiety about their competence, related emotions that have always been conspicuous in the chronicle of human history and have not diminished with the emergence of modern civilization and culture. The greater the concern with politics or with particular governmental policies, the more intense this complex of feelings becomes. Leaders and enemies reinforce each other as the components of the political spectacle that lend it emotional depth as well as the intellectual satisfaction that springs from the transformation of uncertainty, ambivalence, and complexity into an understandable phenomenon.

The term "leader" evokes an ideal type which high public officials try to construct themselves to fit. In this sense leadership is dramaturgy; for regardless of the consequences of officials' actions, which contemporaries cannot know, the ability to create oneself as the ideal type maintains followings. In the age of mass communications dramaturgy has become more central and the pattern it assumes more banal. The leader must be constructed as innovator, as accepting responsibility for governmental actions, as possessing qualities that followers lack, as successful in his or her strategies in contrast to the mistakes of earlier leaders, and, when unsuccessful, as the victim of insuperable obstacles placed there by adversaries or enemies.

In the modern state this portrait of leadership is built up in many ways: the terms of political rhetoric, the construction of historical accounts, the socialization of children and adults, the construction of enemies, problems, and crises, and the planning of the leader's appearance, statements, and gestures. Most of these forms of communication are not intended to mislead, or even to extol leaders. They reflect dominant ideology and reinforce it, and the very absence of self-consciousness about their effects enhances their potency in winning acquiescence in the actions of regimes.

Judgments of Success and Failure

Just as the qualities of leaders are constructed, so also are beliefs about the successes and failures of their policies, for these judgments also hinge upon interpretation and upon ideological definitions of the issues. Assessing governmental performance is not at all like evaluating a plumber by checking whether the faucet still drips. Officials construct tests that show success, just as their opponents construct other tests that show failure. The higher the office the more certain that judgments of performance depend upon efforts to influence interpretations by suggesting which observations are pertinent, which irrelevant, and what both mean.

Even the costs of officials' actions become evidence of their exceptional qualities when publicized through appropriate dramaturgy. Military defeats, to consider a polar example, have often been accepted as demonstrations of leaders' courage and resolution rather than as evidence of misconceived decisions to use force or of strategic incompetence. The fiasco at the Bay of Pigs in 1961 increased President Kennedy's popularity, for it bolstered his image as a decisive leader.[1] Nixon's landslide electoral victory in 1972 as defeat in Vietnam was becoming obvious exemplified the same effect as did the wave of enthusiasm for Gerald Ford's costly and futile use of force in the Mayaguez affair in 1975. Carter, by contrast, publicly recognized his effort to use force to free the hostages in Iran as a tactical defeat, turning the episode into a drama about incompetence rather than an illustration of assertiveness and courage.

Domestic policies that are ruinous to many can similarly be accepted as evidence of effective leadership. Economic policies in the 1980s that helped destroy a high proportion of America's manufacturing industries and farms and sharply increased unemployment, apparently permanently, became evidence of resolute and innovative economic change and helped reelect Reagan overwhelmingly in 1984 with the strong support of many of the farmers, workers, and managers who were displaced. Civil rights and affirmative action policies helped win popularity for Kennedy and Johnson in the sixties, and obstruction or repeal of the same policies helped win popularity for Reagan in the eighties. The explanation for these seemingly paradoxical reactions lies, again, in the inevitable ambiguities that pervade beliefs about the consequences of official actions.

1. *Opinion Polls: Interviews by Donald McDonald with Elmo Roper and George Gallup* (Santa Barbara, Calif., 1962), 34–35.

Leaders construct benchmarks to focus attention where they want it and to create impressions: Camp David peace conferences, military adventures like the Cuban Missile Crisis and the Grenada invasion, alleged drops in the unemployment rate from whatever base period makes the point, enemy body counts, or selected policy proposals. An increase in spending, a relaxation of credit controls, or a dramatic foreign policy move near election day is especially effective, for judgments of success normally depend heavily upon recent developments. Challengers publicize alternative interpretations but find it harder than incumbents to create events that influence opinion.

The construction of a persona can also become a criterion of effectiveness. An ebullient Franklin Roosevelt was a sign to many that the President was making good headway against economic depression and the psychological depression that accompanies it. A folksy warm Reagan signals a trustworthy leader to people who, at another level of awareness, fear that he is trigger happy or suspect that he cares little for the welfare of the poor, minorities, and women.

Leaders, then, are potent symbols for diverting public concern from well-being to constructed happenings. Economic distress, the threat from a foreign power, social unrest, even defeat in war can be turned to the advantage of incumbents who are able to orchestrate public concern so as to focus it upon a reassuring future of ambiguous incidents that are accepted as evidence of successful strategy.

Some officials prove inept at shaping the meanings of developments, or their opponents may be more astute. When that is so, leaders can become symbols of failure. Herbert Hoover was identified with the 1929 stock market crash and the great depression, absorbing responsibility and blame that could have been directed at business mismanagement, mindless stock market speculation, and the inherent risks of finance capitalism. Subordinate officials are often saddled with responsibility for the failures of policies they were administering in line with their superiors' ideologies.

To personify failure in a conspicuous official is to minimize the chance that public restiveness or protest will force institutional change. Individuals are expendable so that established power relationships and modes of allocating resources can continue with minimal challenge in spite of unpopular policies. Judgments of leaders' success or failure, in short, reflect and influence public enthusiasms and public anger, but they do not necessarily reflect the effectiveness of leaders' policies. Officials replace one another and so do political parties that overlap in their ideologies and actions. These publicized alternations, bringing recurring blame for failure and hope for the future, are protectors of ongoing institutions. They signify dynamism and responsiveness to discontents. Lyndon Johnson's assumption of the role of scapegoat in 1968 helped make it possible for his failing policies in Vietnam to continue for another four years.

Beliefs about success and failure are among the most arbitrary of political constructions and perhaps the least likely to be recognized as arbitrary. The issue turns on which actions and which consequences are to be highlighted and which ignored, for every act brings a chain of consequences that help some people and hurt others. The acts that rationalize and perpetuate incumbent leadership are for the most part those that can readily be dramatized; they consist largely of defeats of foreign and domestic enemies and threats. Slow contributions to the well-being of large numbers of people are rarely the stuff upon which leadership is built, and gradual declines in such well-being are easily ignored as well.

In this perspective the actions that create or perpetuate leadership can be disasters for much of the population. Victorious military campaigns mean the death and suffering of friends and relatives. Fiscal and monetary policies that enrich the national treasury may bring unemployment and destitution. The suppression of strikes, riots, and rebellions means defeat, imprisonment, and dreary lives of hard work, malnutrition, and pain, relieved by religion and by bread and circuses in various forms.

The strong leader and the great leader is the most likely to bring such disasters. Though some political leaders help alleviate these problems, most have joined in creating and aggravating them, often winning glory and fame as a result, for leaders' reputations do not hinge upon a ledger account of the consequences of their acts (which, as Hannah Arendt reminded us, can only be known to the historian),[2] but rather upon assaults upon enemies, problems, and crises that are typically constructed for the purpose.

Regimes often claim that they reflect either a common interest or a fair compromise among contending groups, at least in the long run. Whether that posture is hypocritical or sincere, it is typically successful enough to rationalize favoritism for some groups. In the absence of clear indices, observers are tempted to invent some or to project what they want to see. A confident manner, ebullience, an appeal for sacrifice in the public interest, or a narrative account about the past or the future that assuages anxieties readily becomes a substitute for demonstrable improvement in well-being. By the same token complexity, pessimism, or a lack of dramatic talent becomes a reason for disaffection from leaders. Perhaps more blatantly than in any other kind of political judgment, assessments of the performance of leaders are vulnerable to displacement, projection and rationalization.

Do Leaders Make a Difference?

The epistemological and the ontological questions raised by the term "leadership" are complex; successful political maneuver often depends upon confusion about them. A key element is the temptation to praise or blame conspicuous officials for good or ill fortune. The installation of individuals in high governmental office is an invitation to acclaim them for welcome developments and to denounce them for painful and disturbing ones. The very creation of conspicuous governmental offices is very likely attributable in an important sense to the need for personifications to praise and blame. The work of Thomas Carlyle epitomizes that view. For Carlyle the actions of leaders determine the course of events; history is biography.[3] Is that widely shared belief a form of projection or displacement or is it a recognition of the manifest contribution of the leader? The answer hinges upon related issues: the role of the subject and the conditions for achieving and maintaining a position of governmental leadership.

2. Hannah Arendt, *The Human Condition* (Chicago: University of Chicago Press, 1959), 169–70.
3. Thomas Carlyle, *On Heroes, Hero-Worship, and the Heroic in History* (New York: Scribner's Sons, 1901).

Some of the most influential social theories see the very notion of leadership as a misconception. In the Marxist tradition structural conditions determine which forms of leadership will be accepted and what they can accomplish. In late twentieth century structuralist analysis, the individual subject is not the source of action, but only a locus through which structures express their meaning. The poststructuralists define leaders, like all subjects, as a creation of language. In the group theory of Arthur F. Bentley a leader is constituted by the interplay of group interests.[4] These social theories, then, define leadership as an epiphenomenon, a byproduct of more fundamental historical and social processes. But these processes, unlike the leader, are not apparent to the observer without rigorous and imaginative inquiry. The most conspicuous characteristic of leaders, by contrast, is their visibility; they exist to be noticed and to symbolize the actions of governmental bodies, their antecedents and their results.

The conflict between Marx and Carlyle respecting leadership involves ideological, as well as epistemological, issues. To those who see the leader as an epiphenomenon, explanations of politics in terms of leaders' traits and their formal and publicized actions are evasions. They exclude the historical, the economic, and the social conditions that shape wellbeing and consciousness and that must be confronted to bring about meaningful change. In this view a change of leaders is irrelevant, except as mystification, for their successors can only reflect the structural possibilities of the time. These premises are conducive to radical ideologies, for they define economic and political institutions as contingent and as appropriate for reconstruction or abolition.

The idea that history is biography and that political leaders shape the fortunes of peoples and nations, by contrast, justifies itself essentially on empirical grounds. The leader's authority, responsibility, and power are accepted at face value and the view that they reflect more fundamental processes becomes speculation or illusion. This stance discourages attacks on economic and social institutions. It suggests instead that the discontented ought to concentrate on influencing or replacing leaders.

4. Arthur F. Bentley, *The Process of Government* (Cambridge: Harvard University Press, 1908).

Everyday reporting of the political spectacle systematically reinforces the assumption that leaders are critical to the course of governmental action. News accounts highlight the talk and actions of leaders and of aspirants to leadership. They focus upon the election and appointment of high officials and upon policy differences and agreements. Interest groups and governmental agencies feed this kind of news to the media, reinforcing the premise that leadership is central to value allocation and well-being. Only rarely do the media, officials, or interest groups point to historical change in institutions or in material conditions as the explanation of controversial developments. Their focus upon the dramatic current spectacle wins them audiences and support. They thrive upon heroes, villains, contests for votes, legislative and judicial victories and defeats, and especially upon the evocation of leaders with whom people can identify or whom they can blame for their discontents.

So far as the treatment of leadership is concerned, the requisites of explanation and the imperatives of politics and of journalism are in conflict. The texts that tap an interest in spectacle cannot probe the complexities of historical changes in class, national, or other social relationships and consequent reallocations of benefits. There is always an avid interest in the "traits" of leaders, in their personality characteristics, and in stories about their "decisions" and their interactions with others. Picture magazines, newsweeklies, and television and print news media cater to the demand for such accounts.

It finds expression in the academic literature as well in typologies of character and personalities and in studies of "decision-making." The emphasis is upon the leader as the source of ideas and action, either as inventor or as the eminence who chooses among conflicting recommendations. Consider a sentence in James McGregor Burns's book, *Leadership,* that epitomizes both the scholarly and the popular focus: "Napoleon, it is said, could leap upon a battle scene of unimaginable disorder and see its coherence for his own advantage."[5] The arresting claim evokes a hero and spreads his aura to other leaders as well, while the phrase, "it is said," informs readers who choose to notice it that the claim is a legend. The dissemination of such legends helps

5. James McGregor Burns, *Leadership* (New York: Harper Row, 1978), 414.

win acquiescent followers, and one dramatic case suggests that unique talents characterize true leaders in general. Memorable sentences like the one Burns offers us erase from attention everything that helps explain Napoleon's successes except a trait alleged to exist inside his head. It excludes the popular appeal throughout Europe of the French Revolution that Napoleon represented, the faltering efforts of old regimes to obstruct the economic liberties necessary to the development of capitalism, the relative strength, resources, and experience of the French army vis-a-vis its military opponents, the internal schisms and weaknesses of the regimes Napoleon defeated, and so on. Burns does not deny that such considerations are crucial, but his failure to examine them while highlighting a romantic speculation nicely illustrates the capacity of language that is present and of language that is absent to structure beliefs. That example is especially revealing in the light of Tolstoy's interpellations on leadership in *War and Peace,* concluding that even Napoleon could have little insight into effective battlefield strategy and no control over the course of battle. Tolstoy sees a portrayal of leadership in the sense of unique talent as mystification.

The term focuses suspicion on institutions and authority or it legitimizes both. Any text, like Burns's or Tolstoy's, that evokes a pattern of assumptions regarding a particular political figure spreads these assumptions to other contexts and figures as well. Napoleon as guiding genius helps make a unique talent of Julius Caesar and of Franklin Roosevelt.

Dictators, tyrants, and despots appear to be the clearest cases of leaders who do indeed make a difference, but here as well the breadth, depth, and acumen of the analyst's gaze are crucial. Every despot acts in accordance with some sentiments that are widely held, and there are always social or economic groups that benefit from the state's resort to repression. Is it the conjuncture of conditions and ideologies or the personal will of the despot that makes the difference? The tyrant is the symbol of tyranny, but whether he is also the cause hinges upon premises that are always problematic.

Many political leaders who act in controversial fashion are tyrants to some and representatives of the people to others, for their reputations depend upon whose interests focus attention and what consequences are attributed to their actions. Leaders as diverse in ideology and style as Franklin Roosevelt and P.W. Botha of South Africa have been called both tyrants and statesmen. When James MacGregor Burns declares that "a leader and a tyrant are polar opposites,"[6] he is asserting his romanticized view, while ignoring the critical part interpretation plays in all perceptions of leadership.

By the tests democratic theorists apply, there is a crucial distinction between a Roosevelt elected four times through universal suffrage and a Botha who would be rejected overwhelmingly if there were universal suffrage in South Africa. But these two are like each other and like all other political leaders in the respects that bear upon the functions of leaders rather than upon the formal definition of democratic government. The policies of both have reflected the unequal resources available to contending groups, and both are judged to be legitimate leaders or oppressors according to the ideology and social position of the perceiver (even if the perceiver is a social scientist).

The constraint social structure places on leaders can still leave them wide discretion on matters that are not crucial to powerful groups or that are in dispute among influential groups. Sometimes such discretion is decisive. If Hitler kills Jews when other leaders responsive to German antisemitic sentiment would only harass and persecute them, Hitler's discretion is obviously conclusive in its consequences for the Jews. In general, discretionary policies of leaders persist only so long as they remain acceptable to the groups that can apply sanctions. Roosevelt's NRA did not last, and his court packing plan was never enacted. Botha knows he has no discretion to grant broad civil rights to blacks. But until World War II, Hitler's genocidal persecutions were accepted by the German population and by foreign governments without any effective resistance.[7] The exercise of discretion reveals what is

---

6. *Ibid.*, 3.
7. Binion characterizes the occasional anti-Hitler efforts as ". . . paralyzed by telltale passivity, indecision, and blundering." Rudolf Binion, *Hitler among the Germans* (New York: Elsevier Scientific Publishing Co., 1976), 79. Bullock depicts them as ". . . essentially a number of small, loosely connected groups, fluctuating in membership, with no common organization and no common purpose other than hostility to the existing regime." Alan Bullock, *Hitler*, rev. ed. (New York: Harper and Row, 1962), 735. See also Richard Grunberger, *The Twelve-Year Reich* (New York: Holt, Rinehart and Winston, 1971), 39, 111, 142–44.

tolerable and what unacceptable to those who can deploy sanctions.

Not surprisingly, then, discretion is broadest respecting policies that affect weak or powerless people. A proposal to increase unemployment insurance coverage encounters significant resistance if it will also increase employer payroll taxes except when fear of social disruption weakens such resistance; but regimes always enjoy wide discretion to change welfare eligibility rules if they hurt only the potential beneficiaries.

"Do leaders make a difference?" seems to be the wrong question because an affirmative answer is trivial and a negative answer is wrong.

The Creation of Difference and Opposition in Leaders

Whether or not they make a difference, aspirants and incumbents present themselves as unique choices, offering something different from their rivals in style, personality, policies, empathy, or intelligence. A high proportion of their publicized actions and language bear that message, and followers offer it as their rationale for accepting the role.

Reporters and cartoonists reinforce the dramaturgical posture once it is created, highlighting difference through a focus upon physical features, temperament, qualities of mind, nicknames, ideological labels, and characteristic forms of action and speech. Once these symbols are well established, they become scripts for the actors and landmarks for observers.

The phenomenon is revealing, but not because the angle of a cigarette, a distinctive mustache, a folksy optimism, or any such characteristic is important in itself. The straining to signify difference reveals, rather, that politicians recognize essential sameness in what aspirants stand for as the problem. To people who feel deprived or dissatisfied, the contest for political leadership represents a potentiality for change, a promise that discontents will be addressed at their roots. When the alternatives presented for public support are less crucial than concerned groups would like, difference must be constructed, highlighted, or exaggerated.

The effective gesture for creating difference is the constitution of opposition for an incumbent or aspiring leader. There is always a rival who represents a choice, an alternative course for the polity. Even in one-party states and totalitarian states where opposition is prohibited, the leader keeps constantly before the public an evocation of an alternative that has allegedly brought disaster in the past or promises to do so in the future. Political oppositions create each other by invoking the differences between them. Construction of symbols of that difference inevitably follows and helps reify the alternative.

Where ideological differences are slight, leaders and challengers face a dilemma. All of them must use the appeals that win the broadest support, yet they must somehow distinguish themselves from one another. The favored strategy is ambiguity, which avoids offending those who might find a clear promise offensive, encourages everyone to read their own preferences into the language,[8] and at the same time permits speakers to emphasize their difference from rivals by relying on stylistic idiosyncrasies. To supplement ambiguity, attacks on rivals' alleged departures from the modal position, their unreliability, their character, or their ambiguities help create distinctions. But policy differences must remain minor because the optimal strategy for maintaining support is basically the same for everyone. The smaller the differences in action that matter, the more compelled are contenders to employ language that constructs oppositions. Such an emphasis can usually be accepted as an indicator of sameness, a compensation for lack of difference in policy outcomes.

A somewhat similar contradiction holds where there are deep ideological differences, as in the case of leaders of democracies who define themselves in terms of their differences from leaders of dictatorships or from their radical critics. Here the very intensity of the focus upon opposition induces antagonists to act in ways that emulate the other. Democratic leaders become so preoccupied with talk of subversion or invasion that they place a higher priority upon security and regimentation than upon civil rights and public participation. By the same token, despotic leaders worry about the attraction of foreign ideologies and so claim that they are building "true" democracies and may establish a facade of democratic procedures.

8. Benjamin Page, *Choices and Heroes in Presidential Elections* (Chicago: University of Chicago Press, 1979).

Opposition accordingly yields paradox in political leadership. Difference and antagonism grow from impression management, even while they tempt leaders to become more like their opponents. Opposition also yields stability because it mobilizes the concerned public to justify an established position to avoid its replacement by a challenger. In politics, then, the rhetoric of opposition diminishes the prospects for policy change either by incumbents or by their challengers. While creating a spectacle of conflict, it musters public support for leaders and for the interests they represent.

Innovation

The connotation of "innovator" resonates from the term "leader," the person who sets out on an original course that others follow or emulate. Even though few people are likely, if expressly asked, to claim that originality is characteristic of all political leaders, that central significance of the term imbues the actions of leading officials with the aura of innovation. Management, acceptance of the choices of subordinates, dramaturgy, conformity to accepted ideology, even repression, become romanticized as forms of invention.

References to high public officials as "leaders" establishes a dubious link between them and practitioners of other skills in which originality is either the essential avenue to distinction or a fairly common talent: science, the arts, cultural enterprises, some professions, some skilled and unskilled trades. In such activities originality is prized and rewarded. Leaders in one situation are followers in others. Leadership is recognized as an attribute of particular actions, not as an inherent trait of persons and not as a claim to power over other people.

In politics both these expectations are normally reversed. Conformity to the expectations and demands of dominant groups and the public brings support, while innovative ideas are more likely to disqualify an aspirant. Plato, Machiavelli, or Marx do not become political leaders, not, at least, because of their original thought.

Governmental officials are hedged about with constituencies able to block their initiatives or displace them if they threaten influential social groups. Elections, checks from other governmental organs, resistance or refusal to cooperate from allies and subordinates, and, when necessary, rebellion keep political leaders in line.

Much of the time this means that leaders promote adherence to the status quo and must do so as the price of their power, a condition that places a premium upon dramaturgical talent for innovativeness in rhetorical style and in gestures that masks conformity in value allocations. On the rare occasions that a new class or other social grouping is in the process of achieving a dominant position, leaders are constrained to promote change to reflect the new alignment; they fall from power if they do not, as the leaders of the old regimes in France, Russia, and England did during the great revolutions in those countries. Weberian charismatic leaders draw their appeal chiefly from the excitement and euphoria attending such change. In these situations an individual can win a personal following, but no individual can create the prerequisite conditions. In both the static and the revolutionary situations, political leaders are agents able to retain power only if they veto policy proposals that threaten their principals.

Leaders in activities that demand originality use their talents to gratify and educate others, to broaden their horizons, their capacities, and their autonomy. Political leaders, by contrast, use their claim to leadership to justify the exercise of power over others. The difference in meaning and in consequences offers a striking demonstration of the power of an evocative concept to leave traces that distort, in this instance rationalizing subordination in the name of liberation.

What of the occasional leader who is also an original theorist: Woodrow Wilson, Lenin, Mao? These may be the most revealing cases of all, for an examination of their careers makes it evident that the roles of politician and theorist are quite separate. Theorists who become leaders survive by adopting courses of action that reflect the structural possibilities in the situations in which they find themselves, just as other leaders do, even when this means ignoring their innovative ideas. Lenin adopted a "New Economic Policy" restoring capitalist enterprise when he had to. Mao postponed indefinitely the promises in his earlier writings to change the disadvantaged status of women, and he sanctioned repression when threatened. Wilson did display a rather rigid adherence to his academic views about the advantages of parliamentary government and the decisive role of the executive, but his rigidity in failing to take account of congressional opposition led to his defeat on the issue closest to his heart, the Versailles Treaty, and his loss of influence as a political leader.

Prior ideas, whether their own or other people's, may sensitize officials to possibilities or to strategies that would not otherwise occur to them, but in the last analysis, the possibilities in the contemporary situation determine which ideas are appropriate and which must be discarded or altered.

The Construction of Political Innovation

The appearance of innovation is nonetheless almost as necessary for officials who depend upon mass support as is conformity to prevailing ideas and structural possibilities because the spectacle of leaders departing upon new paths establishes their special talent and reinforces their right to rule. The classic devices for constructing the phenomenon of the innovating leader are stylistic play with language and gesture and the publicizing of innovative techniques.

Aspirants for the leadership of nation states differ most strikingly from one another in their talents for deploying phrases and gestures that create a bond with large audiences. The language that becomes memorable is likely to promise security against a feared threat ("All we have to fear is fear itself") to express hostility toward a traditional enemy, to echo common hopes, or to demand sacrifices for the common good ("I offer only blood, sweat, and tears"). Such language forms construct the leader as the exceptional person ready to confront the challenges that intimidate others. At the same time they establish a bond with their audiences by gratifying conscious and unconscious desires, and they promote policies that are consonant with prevailing ideologies.

A focus upon techniques without reconsidering ends also legitimizes leadership. Jürgen Habermas has persuasively argued that discourse about techniques displaces discourse about values.[9] Discourse about techniques maintains a following for political leaders as well by focusing attention upon

9. Jürgen Habermas, *Theory and Practice* (Boston: Beacon Press, 1973), 195–283.

actions hailed as pioneering while obscuring their effectiveness in maintaining the relative power of contending groups.

Technique carries a strong appeal in a capitalist society that socializes people to see inventive methods as the avenue to a better life. An emphasis upon means for administering governmental programs incorporates the aura of rationality associated with the technological progress of industry in the last two centuries.[10] Little wonder, then, that the discussion of public programs and of the leaders who sponsor them concentrates almost exclusively upon techniques and that officials' reputations rise and fall with their promotion of revenue sharing, regulation, deregulation, five year plans, workfare, treaties for regulating the relations among hostile nations, and so on.

Every such technique amounts to an ambiguous, amorphous policy that changes with the pressures of the time and the specific issue. Which people get how much in assistance or in constraints is not defined either by the announcement of a policy or by the political language of its sponsors or its opponents. Techniques and language define an area of contention, a semantic space within which rival groups deploy a conventional set of terms and assumptions; but neither the language nor the formal adoption of a technical policy defines the outcome of the contention, which fluctuates with changes in the resources of the contenders.

Staff Functions

The language and dramaturgy of hierarchies typically understate the contributions of subordinates for everyday decisions and successes, while actions that prove embarrassing are likely to bring reprisals against subordinates. When governmental functions involve diverse treatment of large numbers of individual clients, low level staff make the key decisions. Attendants and nurses in mental hospitals, classroom teachers, probation officers, prison guards, and the staff members of social welfare agencies largely set the quality of life for millions of individuals. The most potent and autocratic controls over individual lives are, in fact, exercised by low-level, low-status staff members whose anonymity protects them from criticism but also deprives them of public credit for praiseworthy performances. These people often

10. Herbert Marcuse, *One Dimensional Man* (Boston: Beacon Press, 1966).

display impressive originality. If innovativeness were in fact the important component of leadership, those subordinates who apply novel ideas and practices would be regarded as political leaders. Instead, the routine functioning of such street-level bureaucracies without too much controversy confers a reputation for leadership upon their immediate heads and also upon the highest officials of the regime.[11]

Most economic, military, and foreign policy decisions are based upon the proposals of subordinates at all hierarchical levels. Conflicts are progressively resolved at higher levels of the organization, so that in most instances the recommendations that reach the chief executive leave little ground for discretion at that level. Policies are announced as the decisions of formal superiors, creating and maintaining their reputations as leaders.

The hierarchical flow of paper, information, and recommendations therefore prevents top officials from acting autonomously or in an original way. Either the need for specialized knowledge or the need for legitimation through specialized knowledge requires the participation of subordinate staff and, in most cases, makes the nominal superior the captive of the analyses of subordinates. A position of "leadership" is a guarantee in most instances that independent judgment and innovative action are impossible.

The organizational straitjacket can be removed, but only in rather rare circumstances. If the social groups that have dominated the state and society are discredited by economic, military, or other failures, the bureaucratic units that have been responsive to those groupings are likely either to be abolished or to gain some discretion to reflect new social formations. The United States Department of Labor underwent such a transformation during the Great Depression of the 1930s, becoming newly responsive to the interests of trade unions. The Office of Economic Opportunity was abolished in the early 1970s with the political decline of constituencies sensitive to the poor and to liberal ideology.

While most executives maintain their political support by reflecting the interests already powerful in the administrative

11. David Mechanic, "Sources of Power of Lower Participants in Complex Organizations," *Administrative Science Quarterly* 7 (December, 1962): 349–64; Michael Lipsky, *Street-Level Bureaucracy* (New York: Russell Sage, 1980).

hierarchies, an occasional leader is sufficiently self-assured and venturesome to play rival groupings against one other and so achieve room for personal maneuver. In view of the bureaucratic domination of contemporary government, only a structural strategy can accomplish this result: the planned jurisdictional overlap of administrative units with conflicting constituencies. A "messy" structure of this kind assures that on crucial issues conflicts will not be resolved inside the bureaucracy and so come to the attention of the chief executive. Franklin Roosevelt used the tactic routinely,[12] and Lyndon Johnson and Winston Churchill sometimes did; but it is probably feasible only at times the public regards as "crises": wars and potentially catastrophic economic and social situations. In this sense, the strategy reflects a social conjuncture rather than a personal executive choice.

The language and the dramaturgical gestures required of subordinates in order to maintain their positions routinely give superiors credit and "responsibility" for decisions and policies, an outcome that is necessary for regime legitimation and for social stability. The code of bureaucratic organizations encourages subordinates and superiors to act as if executives consider a range of suggestions from their subordinates and show their creative acumen in choosing which to accept.

Other organizational practices abet that game: titles, physical arrangements, the presentation of ideas under the aegis and often the signature of the formal head of the organization; the encouragement of hierarchical superiors to act as if the policies they promulgate are their own, with an accompanying dramaturgy of consultation and subordination by staff members; the frequent use of group meetings for the discussion of ideas; the adoption of terms that confound the distinction between innovation and formal responsibility.[13] The more elevated the bureaucratic position the more likely that credit for originality is undeserved, the less possible it becomes to assign credit or blame for results, and the less clear it is what should be counted as success and what as failure. In these subtle ways, the institutional influences that shape bureaucratic policy directions become transformed into an image of individual responsibility.

12. Arthur Schlesinger, Jr., *The Age of Roosevelt* (New York: Houghton Mifflin, 1957).
13. Victor F. Thompson, *Modern Organization* (New York: Knopf, 1961), 138–51.

The Incentive for Inauthenticity

Both the incentive to take positions opportunistically and the means for dishonest public presentations of self have grown markedly in this century. To become and remain a leader in the modern state, a person must win the support of a coalition of disparate and conflicting interests and usually must be elected to office as well. A growing number of interest groups base their support or opposition on a single issue. Many people are attracted by a manner, an optimistic outlook, or a currently fashionable ideology, such as liberalism in the thirties and the sixties and conservatism in the fifties and the eighties. The advent of the electronic media has vastly enhanced the temptation to cater to these pressures quite self-consciously at the cost of candor.

Some degree of inauthenticity is unavoidable in this milieu, and it dominates the life of many politicians. In recent American history, Franklin Roosevelt may represent a fairly innocuous case. The Great Depression facing Roosevelt when he was sworn in as President in March 1933, made it easy for him to be honest about his policies and plans even though they contradicted some of his pre-election claims, such as his promise to balance the budget. With business fearful, subdued, and distrusted, and sympathy for the unemployed and for governmental intervention strong, an even moderately sensitive leader would have found it politic to pursue liberal and mildly reformist positions.

Still, Roosevelt was far more cautious in action than he was in his rhetoric; and often he was deceptive, leading people to believe that he supported their causes even while he encouraged the same confidence in their rivals. He could remain forthright about most of his major policies and promises while still indulging in many lapses from candor, usually through inaction or ambiguity. He repeatedly voiced sympathy for persecuted European Jews while refusing to admit more than a trickle to the United States or to bomb the German extermination camps. This equivocation maintained support for his war policies among right-wing groups and some foreign leaders, a tragic example of dishonesty in the service of expediency.

Inauthenticity has become a far more common feature of the political scene in the years since World War II, an integral aspect of the political system rather than a reflection of individual pathology. In Roosevelt's day, misleading rhetoric was cause for embarrassment when discovered. It has since become a source of pride on many occasions, evidence that a politician is adept at using the system for his advantage. Senator Joseph McCarthy's dramatic success in using lies and unsupported claims to gain a followinging revealed the possibilities, winning him a measure of immunity from criticism and wide support until, several years later, McCarthy had become a caricature of himself, flaunting his power, his arbitrariness, and his willingness to hurt the innocent and so became a threat to other politicians.

Recent presidents have sometimes dramatized the contradictions between their promises and their actions. John Kennedy became a symbol of support for the civil rights movement while appointing many federal judges who could be counted on to obstruct it,[14] and his actions respecting the Bay of Pigs and Vietnam further illustrate the point. Lyndon Johnson won American entry into the Vietnam War by deceiving the Senate and the country into believing that North Vietnam had fired on American ships without provocation. Richard Nixon repeatedly issued misleading statements regarding his peace plans, his foreign policy negotiations, his tactics for dealing with domestic groups he regarded as political enemies, and the reasons for domestic unrest. Ronald Reagan has misled the country about the effects upon the poor of his tax reductions and his cuts in social programs, about the human rights records of foreign governments he supports, and about his administration's responsibility for deficits and for unemployment. All regimes since World War II have been deceitful about CIA actions to undermine foreign governments. Deception has become a public relations gambit rather than an ethical lapse. The more exalted the office and the more disparate the groups to be courted, the more institutionalized it becomes.

To become a political leader entails a particular kind of self-conception and an opportunistic scale of values. Power easily becomes an end in itself, to be sought by any means that can be rationalized or concealed, a perversion of Machiavellian strategy.

14. Jack F. Peltason, *Fifty-eight Lonely Men* (New York: Harcourt, Brace, and World, 1961).

Those who are willing to assume that kind of role try to become leaders, and the public is increasingly socialized to accept the role as legitimate and necessary, even admirable. Leaders doubtless justify their political performances to themselves as instrumental in accomplishing worthy goals, and they differ in some measure in naming their objectives; but the names of goals remain tactics for courting support rather than conditions to be sought.

Inauthentic performance creates deep ambivalence in the public. It generates profound skepticism about political promises and accomplishments, so that support grows more erratic. But political promises and threats remain in a separate universe of discourse from well-being. That is the central paradox of contemporary liberal states, the phenomenon that American leaders began to understand and to exploit in a blatant way in the latter half of the twentieth century: with McCarthy's talent for creating fear without evidence that it was warranted and with John Kennedy's promises of a new youth and glory for America that had no relation to current conditions or to his administration's policies.

With Reagan the new leadership strategy became self-conscious and unprecedentedly successful, offering a "safety net" for the poor that legitimized a large increase in poverty and homelessness and verbal support for a "balanced budget" and even for a balanced budget amendment that provided a soothing obbligato to the creation of deficits exceeding all previous ones in American history combined.

There is a psychological explanation for the political success of language that contradicts policies and readily observable current conditions. People who are anxious, fearful, and discouraged about the conditions of their lives respond with hope and enthusiasm to unambiguous promises to improve those conditions and also to clear definitions of enemies responsible for their deprivations. The leader who persuasively offers such promises and definitions becomes a hero; the public that identifies with his or her expressed hopes and fears is now inclined to attribute their misfortunes to political enemies rather than to his failures, contradictions, or hypocrisy. Failure in performance can become the avenue to political success. Deprivation and anxiety can foster credibility and gullibility.

Though blatant contradiction may be new as a self-conscious

political strategy in the liberal democracies, it has a long history of having constructed popular leaders. The demagogue who plays upon people's misfortunes to win their allegiance through promises of a happy future that will not be realized is a recurring historical figure. The artful use of television and radio to bring leaders close to their audiences has extended the possibilities of a classic form of power seeking.

Leadership as Exclusion

The main function of "leadership" as a sign is to displace from attention most of the structural influences, conflicts, unequal bargains, strategies, repressions, tensions, and failures characteristic of politics. To focus upon an individual setting the policy course which many follow and some resist is to erase the changes in material and cultural conditions that determine which individuals and policies are viable and which doomed to defeat. This may be the fundamental exclusion, and it provides the setting for others as well.

The language of "leadership" reduces a complex and historically dynamic scene to individual traits and actions. It displaces key social psychological phenomena from attention as well: the need of opponents for a leader to attack and the need of loyal supporters for a leader to praise. Both followers and antagonists require that leadership be constructed so that a conspicuous individual or oligarchy can be invested with personal authority and responsibility.

This displacement is crucial for understanding motivation and incentive, for it diminishes both moral responsibility for the dubious actions of governments and blame for the failures of government. People who would never kill, cause suffering, or act in grossly unfair ways in the parts of their lives they define as private are sometimes eager to support these actions when the responsibility is transferred to official leaders. The psychological process of displacement is all the more useful when such policies bring material benefits or gratify biases, as they often do.

Political leaders enjoy a considerable measure of immunity from the moral principles that are applied, inconsistently, to everyone else. Some special bits of language convert immoral action into the promotion of the public interest, the act of state, the assertion of national sovereignty, the effort to balance the budget. These phrases, and others like them, can transform such actions as impoverishing large numbers of people, killing or maiming foreigners, refusing to heed the pleas of the desperate, or contaminating the environment, into evidence of effective leadership.

Leadership, then, is a remarkable sign, blurring history, contemporary social, economic, and psychological interactions, and personal guilt, while substituting an absorbing narrative in their place.

Leadership and Sexism

It is evident from the popular response to many official actions that identification with chauvinist uses of power is common and that officials and aspirants to power are therefore encouraged to adopt it as a strategy. Sexism and chauvinism are implicated in virtually all political processes, dealing as they do with subordination, alliances, the forging and breaking of relationships, aggression against the weak, and, on occasion, with compassion, bonding, and helping others. Prevailing sexist norms influence both support for political leaders and the forms of action that are politically acceptable. It is doubtless one consequence of this phenomenon that political leaders are overwhelmingly males. Closely related is the inclination of the females who become heads of state to develop reputations for chauvinism[15] It is as if women can prove their fitness for high office only by demonstrating their allegiance to patriarchal norms. In their actions and in their talk, political leaders are prone to stress the values of authority, hierarchy, toughness, and dominance over compassion, equality, or the welfare of the powerless, and there is evidence that the public has been socialized to display the same priorities when choosing among aspirants for high office.

Chauvinistic leadership accordingly helps establish a bond between leaders and a substantial part of the population, presumably disproportionately male, though the evidence on that point is inconclusive. Officials who refuse to act chauvinistically are likely to be defined as weak, ineffective, and vulnerable to attack.

15. The twentieth-century record offers few if any counterexamples. Consider the cases of Margaret Thatcher, Golda Meir, Indira Ghandi, and Jean Kirkpatrick, whose chauvinsist stance made her a widely discussed presidential hopeful.

Chauvinism therefore helps in some measure to protect leaders from opposition. It frees them from constraints and it cultivates hubris: a sense of superiority and pride in office that encourages self-centeredness and obliviousness to the concerns of those who suffer from their policies. In this way the power and discretion available to leaders complement the frustrations and discontents of followers and reinforce both. In an important sense leadership is an expression of the inadequate power of followers in their everyday lives.

But it is also a reaction to the inability of leaders to produce the results they and their followers hope to accomplish. In the face of structural constraints they repeatedly find themselves ineffective or impotent; but they can resort to *techniques* that signify power and domination of the polity: war, tough posturing, insensitivity to the powerless. Leaders must repeatedly compromise their principles and causes and often must betray them. In this perspective, chauvinism is a way of concealing their weakness from themselves as well as others. Compromise may be democratic, but it is also humbling unless masked by gestures that symbolize strength.

The Choice among Individual Aspirants

This discussion has said little about the reasons one individual rather than another becomes a political leader. Indeed, it implies that that is not an important question except to aspirants for leadership and their clients.

An analysis of why some individuals win the chance to secure a political following while most of the population never does must begin with the reasons most are excluded. So far as the American presidency is concerned, for example, the entire population except for male WASPS (white Anglo-Saxon Protestants) has been excluded by political party policy or law through most of American history and, except for Catholics, that large majority remains excluded today. Similar legal and cultural exclusions are found in every country, though, as in America, they are often denied by cherished myths like the story that every American child has a chance to grow up to become president.

At the time at which a new head of state is to be chosen it is often organizational talents that prove crucial, even though they are usually not enough to win and retain a following once a person achieves the office. In the United States and in most democratic countries preconvention organization is decisive in winning a party nomination and in one-party states it is equally decisive, though different tactics come into play there. The history of the Soviet Union is an object lesson in that principle, beginning with Lenin's organizational work while in exile and continuing with Stalin's displacement of Trotsky after Lenin's death because Stalin had placed his followers in key positions in the Party. Organizational tactics proved crucial as well after the deaths of Stalin, Krushchev, and Brezhnev. Some who achieve office through this strategy become leaders, and many never do; but events that explain individual accession have little bearing on value allocations.

That point is especially clear in the large number of cases in which party activists exert pressure to seek high office on well-known people with no record of political activity or policy espousal. Successful generals are automatically considered for the presidency, as was the first astronaut to orbit the earth and the president of an automobile manufacturing company that pioneered in building a small car. For political party bureaucrats and aspirants for lower-level offices the top name on the ticket disseminates an appealing aura that can be projected flexibly onto fellow candidates and onto the policies of influential groups.

A party oligarchy occasionally accepts an aspirant for leadership whose policy stands are clear, though such clarity usually invites defeat because it alienates potential voters who dislike the candidate's positions. The landslide defeats of Barry Goldwater in 1964 and George McGovern in 1972 are prototypical. Not specificity but ambiguity is likely to augment a candidate's appeal; and appeal, not ideology, makes a leader useful to a party. Political leaders are most helpful when they can represent whatever meaning concerned groups want to see in them.

The most revealing cases involve "leaders" who make no effort to take part in the movement they allegedly influence. Martin Luther vigorously disavowed any sympathy with the German peasants who rebelled in his name, but the latter saw themselves as his followers and their cause as his. Historians often conclude, as noted earlier, that no identifiable person started or led urban riots, but both the police forces that try to put down the riot and the people who participate in it invariably find "leaders" to whom they attribute responsibility.[16] In such cases the construction of leaders to meet other people's needs is evident. In the more common situation in which the leadership role is accepted rather than rejected, the construction of the leader as symbol is not so obvious, but the psychological dynamics for followers are essentially the same.

Once aspirants for leadership become incumbents, some of the ambiguity about their policies disappears and so, typically, does a corresponding share of their popularity. The ability to attract or hold a following now hinges upon developments that are unique to the particular time. A domestic or foreign crisis is invaluable in maintaining the leader's symbolic appeal even if his or her policy stands are quite clear, as Roosevelt demonstrated throughout his long tenure of the presidency and as Margaret Thatcher's Faulklands adventure proved again.

There is, then, no reason to conclude that policy positions or idiosyncratic talents are critical to the winning of a following except as these skills include a penchant for encouraging people to project their wishes and hopes onto the leader's persona. In retrospect those who have held leadership roles seem to have been the obvious choice rather than the beneficiaries of luck, opportunism, demographic traits, and psychological projection. That the receding political scene takes on the appearance of inevitability is still another example of the effect of immediate involvement upon perception, for the longer the observer's historical perspective and the deeper his or her social perspective, the more apparent it becomes that the accession to leadership of any individual was neither fated nor dependent on specific talents for governing.

Conclusion

The term "leadership" (like the terms "problem" and "enemy") is itself a political weapon. It catalyzes an intricate language game that draws its appeal from a complex of psychological needs including an incentive to blame or praise identifiable people for changes in well-being and an effort to understand why changes take place.

16. Murray Edelman, *Politics as Symbolic Action* (New York: Academic Press, 1971), 120–22.

There is an important sense in which leaders deserve praise and blame for the conditions in which people live. They do identify themselves with particular courses of action and inaction and so deserve responsibility for them. But the assumption that leaders have caused the events for which they take responsibility is reductionist because it ignores the consequences of historical developments, material conditions, and interpretations of those conditions. Except as minor elements of a complex transaction, leaders cannot provide security or bring about change. Their posture of doing so confounds both understanding and public policy.

4 The Construction and Uses of Political Enemies

Because politics involves conflict about material advantages, status, and moral issues, some people are always pitted against others and see them as adversaries or as enemies. Political enemies may be foreign countries, believers in distasteful ideologies, groups that are different in any respect, or figments of the imagination; in any case, they are an inherent part of the political scene. They help give the political spectacle its power to arouse passions, fears, and hopes, the more so because an enemy to some people is an ally or innocent victim to others.

Sometimes political enemies hurt their opponents, and often they help them. Because the evocation of a threatening enemy may win political support for its prospective targets, people construct enemies who renew their own commitment and mobilize allies: witches in seventeenth-century Salem, communists in the army in the 1950s, Jews in Nazi Germany, homosexuals, a foreign regime identified with an unpopular ideology, dissident peasants in Vietnam or El Salvador. When an enemy hurts, there is an incentive to end the threat by doing away with him. But the opposite incentive comes into play when the enemy helps marshal support for a regime or a cause; in that case those who construct an enemy have every reason to perpetuate and exaggerate the threat he poses.

When a claim that a group is dangerous is politically divisive, the claim is likely to depend less upon observation than upon assumptions that cannot persuasively be tested: that nuclear freeze advocates or guerillas in a remote country are dupes of Russian plans for aggression, that employers systematically deprive workers of part of the value of what they produce, that "secular humanists" are destroying the nation's moral fiber. Those who fear enemies are likely to impute traits to them that make them dangerous. That is also the implicit premise of some academic and medical writing, though here it takes the form of assumptions about such unobservables as national character, a culture of poverty, or a psychopathic personality.

Enemies and Adversaries

Opponents in politics are not necessarily enemies, for some opponents are respected and accepted as legitimate. The distinction between unacceptable and acceptable opponents, or between enemies and adversaries, lies in whether the focus of attention is upon the inherent nature of the antagonist, or, instead, upon the tactics an opponent employs.

The world of the game defines the antagonist as an adversary. Here there is competition to win. It may be sporting and good humored, as in many electoral rivalries and some competitions for such public benefits as a new post office or a public contract. It may be deadly serious, as in contested elections, international territorial disputes, and even war. So long as the focus is on finding and pursuing winning tactics, the opponent is an adversary, whether the stakes are small or vast.

The relation between law enforcers and people accused of violations is typically adversarial in this sense. The police officer and the speeder, the factory inspector and the manager who violates a health and safety code, even the prosecutor and the person accused of homicide, are involved in a competitive game in the crucial sense that the costs, the stakes, and even the definitions of the offense are negotiable within some limits, and each party can calculate the probable risks and benefits of pursuing alternative courses of action. In all such encounters there is some sporting element in playing the game and trying to win, and the procedures themselves capture attention.

Where an opponent is an enemy rather than an adversary, it is not the process but the character of the opponent that focuses attention. Enemies are characterized by an inherent trait or set of traits that marks them as evil, immoral, warped, or pathological and therefore a continuing threat regardless of what course of action they pursue, regardless of whether they win or lose in any particular encounter, and even if they take no political action at all. To the Nazi, the Jew is an enemy (and vice versa) so long as he or she exists. When defined as subversive, the liberal is an enemy. So is the foreign country that is perceived as intent upon subverting the "free world" (or the "people's democracies"). If enemies are not observably doing anything, that is itself evidence of underground activities to undermine the good society. In this form of construction, the incentive is not to win encounters but rather to destroy the opponent.

Different kinds of statements are accepted as appropriate for these radically different perceptions of antagonists. To define political opponents as adversaries connotes that the issue is tactical rather than moral; questions of principle and value rankings are not at issue, so that people can decide on the basis of their interests whether to get involved and on which side. The fight is limited in its importance and in the spectrum of groups that are concerned. To define political antagonists as enemies drastically broadens both the range of issues and the range of concerned groups.

Clearly, there is nothing distinctive or inherent about adversaries or enemies as people that makes them one or the other. To understand such language in politics it is necessary to focus upon the social situation and self-characterization of observers rather than upon the people who are labeled. Only then can we explain why changes occur so often in the definitions of political enemies and why, in some situations, *anyone* is likely to define others as enemies or to be defined as such. Many political "enemies" already cited as examples did no harm at all, though the attribution of harm served a purpose for their antagonists.

Political Coalitions

The linking of diverse issues through language about the nature of an enemy who somehow combines them is a common political phenomenon and a potent maneuver for winning support for causes, whether or not it is a conscious tactic. Such linking may be an element in all forms of political coalition building. The portrayal of the poor as enemy helps build an alliance of people who resent using tax money for public assistance, who identify poverty with crime in the streets or with radicalism, or who see the poor as a cultural, moral, or genetic threat to the respectable classes. To personify an issue by identifying it with an enemy wins support for a political stand while masking the material advantages the perception provides.

Such linking of disparate interests through the attribution of feared traits to problematic enemies lends intensity to common causes and sometimes creates a belief in nonexistent common interests. The steel corporation and steelworkers union that join in opposition to foreign steel imports share a clearly recognizable antagonist. Yet the focus on the foreign threat also displaces an alternative explanation: that the problems of American workers do not spring from the hostility of individual foreigners but from the logic of a national and international economy that pits workers against their counterparts abroad and so imports and exports unemployment and wage depression. A dubiously conceived enemy inhibits understanding of a damaging problem and in doing so undergirds a political alliance.

In that example the foreign steel producers do indeed hurt, though they may not be the ultimate enemy. In many other cases political alliances are built upon the construction of enemies who either do not exist or are not harmful to those who label them. Nisei Americans on the West Coast at the time of Pearl Harbor were depicted as a potentially treasonous enemy, a construction that united nationalists and racists and also attracted to the coalition people who would benefit from the forced sale of Nisei property before their owners were herded into camps. The dubious perception of Japanese Americans as dangerous to security was very likely not a conscious lie on the part of those who held it, but rather something far more common and more potent in politics: the construction of an enemy who serves people's interests by winning them wealth, status, or ideological justification.

The intensification of long-standing hostilities may also cement and broaden political alliances. Supporters of larger arms appropriations and of a strategy of confrontation in both the Kremlin and the Pentagon win wider public support at home by publicizing and exaggerating their antagonist's arms increases, aggressive preparations, and intentions. In this crucial sense hawks in rival countries help build domestic political coalitions for their antagonists by pursuing their own goals; and proponents of détente in rival countries help each other in the same way. In this process informal political coalitions can *include* enemies when their aim is to extract larger appropriations and influence through domestic public opinion. In polarizing public opinion, enemies paradoxically cooperate with each other, though the cooperation may be unintentional. The same kind of escalation of tension often enables rivals in domestic politics to help each other while further polarizing opinion. As labor-management tensions escalate, unions typically win more staunch support from their rank and file members and management groups increase their support from stockholders and conservatives. As confrontations between civil libertarians and advocates of crackdowns on criminals grow more intense, public opinion polarizes, and both positions gain in monetary support and in status. The link between social cohesiveness and fear of enemies is therefore an intriguingly dialectical one: division and consensus go hand in hand, with some cleavages cementing others while deepening themselves.[1]

If a widely publicized event can be interpreted as confirmation that a conspicuous enemy is dangerous, a political coalition can usually be broadened. When Russia shot down a Korean airliner carrying 267 passengers in 1983, the officials of the Reagan administration who spoke in public of their anger and revulsion at the action also benefited from the occurrence of an event that could be used to mobilize public support for defeating a nuclear freeze resolution in Congress, building the MX missile, and increasing the arms budget. The sinking of the battleship Maine in 1898 and the siege of the Alamo in 1836 served a similar function, marshalling support among the apathetic for controversial actions by inculcating fear of an enemy. When such interpretations of ambiguous events are widely accepted, the event itself becomes a condensation symbol and can be used to build support for later military actions. The slogans "Remember the Alamo," "Remember the Maine," and "Remember Pearl Harbor" not only broadened support for the wars in which they were early incidents. Taught to children in history courses and cited in patriotic oratory, they continue to reinforce the assumption that military ventures are an effective way to protect the country. They help keep alive a latent coalition that any regime can activate.

It is apparent that in helping to build coalitions, enemies win material gains for those who construct them. The ideology, the material incentive, and the language that evokes them are facets of the same transaction.

---

1. I examined this process in *Politics as Symbolic Action* (New York: Academic Press, 1971), 16–17.

Ambivalence

While beliefs about enemies are typically intense, they are seldom consistent with other political perceptions and are often in conflict even with concurrent beliefs about enemies expressed by the same individual. They must be understood as stock stories exercising influence when the appropriate cues are present. People take the roles of alternative "significant others" in different situations. When attention is directed to the Bolshoi ballet, joint space exploration, or grain sales, an American may see Russia as a friendly power, but perceive the U.S.S.R. as the enemy when focusing upon MX missiles in Idaho or cruise missiles in Europe. We learn stereotyped beliefs as we acquire a culture. In every case a minority, usually small, feels so intensely that there is little occasion for conflicting cognitions; but most of the population displays a substantial measure of ambivalence. Individuals reflect social currents, even when the currents flow in opposite directions.

In international politics it is usually easy to redefine a current ally as an enemy and vice versa and to win widespread public support for the fast switch. At the end of World War II our Russian ally was suddenly converted into the enemy in a cold war while our German enemy just as quickly became an ally. Relations with China underwent a dramatic reversal in 1970. Such Orwellian changes do not occur with respect to any issue on which public opinion is strongly polarized but, paradoxically, when there is something close to a consensus; for in that situation the cues are likely to come from the same source, often the government, and opinion responds to them with little challenge.

Ambivalence is expressed as well through emulation of some of the enemy's actions, a phenomenon that appears regularly at late stages of the historical development of animosities between groups. Perhaps its most easily recognized manifestation is in the tendency of rival national regimes to imitate each other in building weapons systems, making claims about the other's aggressive plans, suppressing domestic criticism and liberties in the name of security, and fashioning their foreign policies as mirror images of one another.

The effect also appears among oppressed groups in domestic politics. They often develop internal factions that fight one another with the same violent methods employed against them by the oppressor. The infighting among blacks and between blacks and Indians in South Africa is a current example of this phenomenon, which appears as well in the willingness of members of oppressed groups to serve as police agents and quislings. Enmity is a bond as well as a divider. Perhaps the most significant political consequence of this form of emulation lies in its power to create a whole set of social transactions in the image of the group that first treats another as an enemy. The discursive constitution of enmity, aggression, and emulation become part of a single process.

A revealing form of ambivalence appears in the ways society deals with people who are normally spoken of with affection and compassion but who are treated in many situations as though they are dangerous, immoral, and incompetent to live autonomous lives. Among these are women, children, some workers and servants, welfare recipients, and nonconformists labeled as mentally disturbed. Together, such groups comprise a large part of the population; the larger the proportion, the more likely they are to be dealt with as enemies. Their status and their treatment vary in different cultures, but they are vulnerable everywhere to exploitation in work and in benefits, denial of rights and opportunities others routinely enjoy, and severe forms of discipline that are typically called "helping."[2]

In these cases the disjunction between language and other actions is striking but is ordinarily not noticed or denied when political dissidents or academic observers call attention to it. These groups are different from those who are explicitly labeled as enemies in two key respects. First, they are in close contact with the rest of the population. Second, their cooperation is vital to the continued functioning of the social order; it is not their hostility (as in the case of other enemies) but their services and sacrifices, that society needs to maintain itself. The language of affection, pity, compassion, and helping masks from the self and from others the importance of exploiting these groups for the maintenance of the social order. This ambivalent form of enmity therefore continues indefinitely, while other types come and go with changes in political needs and opportunities.

2. See my *Political Language* (New York: Academic Press, 1977), chap. 4, for an extended analysis of this phenomenon.

The Linguistic Evocation of Enemies

Beliefs in political enemies seem to influence public opinion most powerfully when the enemy is not named explicitly, but evoked through an indirect reference. Perhaps the most common form of subtle evocation is the advocacy of a course of action that implies that a particular group is dangerous. Any reference to capital punishment, for example, is also a reference to the need to restrain blacks and the poor from violence. The liberal argument that poor people and blacks are disproportionately targeted by capital punishment laws doubtless fuels this fear in a part of the public. That the association is subtle makes it all the more potent, for "capital punishment," like all condensation symbols, draws its intensity from the associations it represses. For many, a reference to slums or to the poor is associated with a dangerous class of people rather than with economic misfortune. Joseph Gusfield has shown that for rural fundamentalists the issue of prohibition of intoxicating beverages evoked a belief in the threat urban Catholics posed to a moral way of life in America.[3] Implicit associations with an enemy lend emotional intensity to a public issue, while the explicit naming of an enemy makes it easier for the opposition to rebut the premise and create some self doubts among those who accept it. Evocation through condensation symbolism is therefore critical to these forms of enemy construction.

The crude and strident language often used to depict enemies also reinforces a latent set of meanings. Resort to terms like "spic," "nigger," and "kike" to refer to minority groups; obscene and scatological language (like that in Julius Streicher's paper, *Der Stürmer,* in the twenties and thirties); references to foreign peoples as barbarians and to foreign states in such terms as Reagan's phrase, "the evil empire," seem to be an effort to go beyond the limits of the conventional vocabulary in order to voice the speaker's hate.

While such language ostensibly depicts its referent as the enemy, it is directed as well against people who fail to share its point of view. To use a term like "nigger" is to challenge the

3. Joseph R. Gusfield, *Symbolic Crusade* (Urbana: University of Illinois Press, 1963).

ideology of humanists and liberals and to associate them with the named enemy. In such cases the implicit target may account for more of the emotional intensity a term evokes than the explicit one, for the naming of blacks as an inferior race amounts to no more than a gratifying reaffirmation of an article of faith, while the implicit claim that advocates of dignity and equal rights for blacks are pathological is self-evidently a challenge. Such language therefore appeals or repels in accordance with its audiences' current values. It polarizes more than it converts. By intensifying the debate it makes the issue more salient and attracts support and resources for both sides. The veiled reference may create ambivalence in liberals while the crude reference intensifies their liberalism.

Language about political enemies is drawn from a rather small set of contradictory and ambiguous propositions that are applied regardless of whether the highlighted difference turns on color, ethnicity, gender, race, class, ideology, or nationality. From a stock pool of claims that evoke suspicion and hostility, those most likely to forge a coalition in the particular case dominate discourse, constructing both the self and the other for people who become involved in the game.

Consider the more contradictory claims. Members of the group in question are aloof and clannish and they insist on entering social circles where they are not welcome. They are less intelligent, lower on the scale of evolution, or farther from God's grace than others and are shrewd, dangerously resourceful, and uncanny in their talent for besting others unless kept in their place by force. They are ill-favored physically, behave like one or another animal, and smell bad, and they display superior sexual attractions and physical talents that make them seductive. They are weak, self-effacing, and cowardly and they are domineering, with a gift for attack or a talent for ruthless tactics.

The effectiveness of ambiguous and contradictory statements in shaping both political encounters and value allocations through the state calls into question the view that the ego can usefully be conceived as continuing or consistent, just as it calls into question the utility of conceiving the social world as a consistent entity. Enemies become whatever claim works for the situation and the moment, subjects and objects become whatever the acceptance of a particular claim makes of them, and neither form of becoming has much bearing upon earlier, concurrent, or subsequent forms, except in the sense that material inequalities influence all of them and so perpetuate some for long periods of time.

The Loss of Perspective

There is typically little correspondence between the measures people take against political enemies and the harm the latter do. It is as if the language of enmity erases reasonable calculation and perspective and overwhelms consciousness. Consider the stereotypes of Japanese character widely accepted in the United States during World War II and how quickly they faded from public consciousness after VJ Day.

A focus on enemies often means loss of perspective as well about justifiable defense measures against them. The ultimate case may be the willingness in some circles to use nuclear weapons against an enemy in order to safeguard national sovereignty even if such use carries a likelihood of destroying that sovereignty and all humanity as well. For a time it was common in some American states to sentence people convicted of possession of small amounts of marijuana to prison for as long as forty years, an action manifestly related to an assumption about inherent evil in the person rather than to the harm that comes from smoking pot. Savage tortures have been inflicted throughout history upon people regarded as religious infidels or as enemies of the state because of their failure to subscribe publicly to a currently fashionable ideology. Punishments are all the more severe when the grounds for believing people do evil are invisible: attributed to the psyche or inherent character rather than to behavior and its observable consequences. Witness the witch burnings of the seventeenth century and the witchhunts of the twentieth. Consider the observation of the American captain in Vietnam that he had to burn a village in order to save it and the remark of a Salvadoran army officer in 1982 that he had to kill women and children because the women were giving birth to infants with the seeds of rebellion in them. There is a perverse rationality at work here. Because there is no limit on the implications of the unobservable, wishful thinking and ideology win free reign.

Justifications of enmity take the form of constructing a

narrative about the past and the future: a story plot that rationalizes draconian measures against supposed enemies on the ground that an evil must be destroyed in order to save the public and the enemies themselves for a better future. To burn heretics, destroy their careers, or publicly humiliate them is to save the social order from contamination and to cure a pathology in the antagonist.

In constructing such enemies and the narrative plots that define their place in history, people are manifestly defining themselves and their place in history as well; the self-definition lends passion to the whole transaction. To support a war against a foreign aggressor who threatens national sovereignty and moral decencies is to construct oneself as a member of a nation of innocent heroes. To define the people one hurts as evil is to define oneself as virtuous. The narrative establishes the identities of enemy and victim-savior by defining the latter as emerging from an innocent past and as destined to help bring about a brighter future world cleansed of the contamination the enemy embodies.

The official definition of a foreign or an internal enemy is sometimes widely disputed, as it was during the Vietnam War and the McCarthy period and is in Central America in the 1980s. Such cases evoke rising dissent, repression of dissidents, and polarized opinion. Disputed definitions of the nature of threats typically flow from ideological rigidity on the part of a regime or from domestic problems that make foreign diversions attractive. To dissenters from official policy the regime itself becomes the threat, while dissenters are more and more intensely attacked in official statements. After a time they may evoke more passionate hostility than the formally defined enemy.

In both the Vietnam War and the McCarthy period the issues were ultimately resolved paradoxically. The view that the official definition of the enemy was misconceived came to be accepted by a high proportion of the population, forcing an end to the disputed policies. Yet the regimes suffered little except perhaps to their reputations in history, while those who had challenged them suffered severely, and some continued to suffer in later years through loss of their jobs, interruptions to their careers, and the association of their dissent with radicalism and irresponsibility. The choice people make between controversial enemies seems to be taken as an indicator of their reliability and respectability, though the accuracy of their choice, as revealed by history, seems to have little bearing so far as dominant public opinion is concerned.

The intense focus upon a political enemy brings with it an impressive sensitivity to some of his or her potentialities and an equally striking insensitivity to others.[4] Strong feeling involves an emotional bond, positive or negative, with one's child, lover, therapist, or antagonist, so that each person grows alert to traits that strengthen or weaken the other. Because Joseph McCarthy was often more sensitive to the ambiguities of liberal rhetoric and liberal causes than the liberals themselves, he could effectively depict liberals as soft on communists. In the same way, the liberals who came to detest McCarthy recognized his willingness to invent data and the personal insecurity and ambition that underlay his posturing better than his sympathizers did. The sensitivity to others that springs from hostility helps tactically in finding their weaknesses and in hurting their causes.

Such knowledge, nonetheless, is double-edged. Its obverse side is diminished attention to differences among the people labeled the enemy, obliviousness to individual diversities and distinctions so as to focus upon the one characteristic or role that constitutes a symbol of threat: a common color, religion, ideology, or nationality. Other differences in talents, interests, political philosophies, and attitudes are muted once a group is defined as the enemy. Germans, Vietnamese, Hispanics, or political dissidents become homogeneous collectivities, no longer distinguished by disparities in values, personalities, politics, or actions. Such distinctions either remain invisible or are accepted as misleading appearances that conceal a basic sameness.

To recognize individuals as human beings, then, is to ignore them as enemies. The anti-Semite who tells you that some of his best friends are Jews can mean it. The psychological disjunction between human beings and enemies also explains how anti-Semitism can be widespread and intense in countries like contemporary Austria in which few Jews live any more. Flesh-and-blood Jews are irrelevant. The day to day actions of real

---

4. *Cf.* Kenneth Burke, *A Grammar of Motives,* (New York: McGraw-Hill, 1945), 6–7.

people in Vietnam or El Salvador similarly had no bearing on whether they posed a "threat to the free world." Stereotyped language creates its own universe of discourse and its own logic. Empathy with the enemy serves a tactical function, for it facilitates exploitation of weaknesses, while insensitivity to individual distinctions serves a propaganda function, for it focuses attention upon the trait that can be used to mobilize allies.

Displacement of Targets

Once we recognize that enmity lies in the eye of the perceiver and that that eye often is not trained upon the supposed enemy's behavior at all, it becomes evident that there need be no logical or empirical link between the experience of grievance and the attribution of a cause for it. People who are denied what they think they deserve or see a threat to their privileges are likely to identify enemies who are allegedly responsible for their grievances; but those who are so named may be innocent in the eyes of historians and social scientists. The displacement of resentments onto personified targets who are vulnerable and available for political and psychological use is pervasive in enemy construction. This often means displacement from those who hurt to those who are politically weak. Sometimes it means displacement onto a foreign country, a religion, or an ideological grouping that symbolizes the alien or the uncanny.

Whether or not such displacement is justified, it is gratifying, for it offers a way to vent discontents onto a target that can usually do little to retaliate. Displacement also makes it unnecessary to undertake any analysis that would probe the part played by social and economic conditions and institutions in unequally allocating life chances, successes, and failures. Unemployment and low real wages generate animus against welfare recipients, blacks, and women, who are blamed for draining the public treasury and for taking the jobs of white males. A large part of the general public is always more ready to blame price inflation on wage demands than on restrictive monetary policies or administered pricing by corporate management, even in industries that are capital intensive.

The highlighting of foreign enemies to weaken domestic dissent or divert attention from domestic problems is a classic political gambit because it is so often an effective one. While this form of displacement is occasionally deliberate, it need not be. That the chronic domestic issues usually involve demands for reforms in the interest of the disadvantaged while foreign problems typically justify governmental expenditures that benefit business groups doubtless helps explain the tendency for liberals to focus upon domestic problems while conservatives prefer foreign threats; but in neither case is the preference likely to be a self-conscious ploy to advance liberal or conservative ideologies. Here, rather, is another example of the capacity to rationalize any policy demands while masking their self-serving character.

But foreign ventures sometimes create domestic unrest rather than end it, as the Vietnam War dramatically illustrated. The crucial question is the degree of public consensus on whether the external enemy a regime attacks is indeed a threat. Public opinion was polarized on that issue respecting Vietnam. In such situations, especially when the military venture is failing, regimes are tempted to see dissenters as giving aid to the enemy and to harass or repress them as best they can, another example of displacement. The Nixon administration's Cointel project was a blatant, if covert, yielding to such temptation, but it more commonly takes the forms of using punitive force to put down demonstrations and of prosecuting dissenters.

A common displacement entails blaming victims of social misfortune for their own troubles: portraying the poor, sufferers from emotional and mental distress, or drug abusers as dangerous people whose moral inadequacies make them responsible for their own problems. While social scientists are more likely to define these people as victims of a world they never made, the attribution of responsibility is sufficiently complex that ideology plays a major part in its perception.

The form of displacement that is most supportive of political and social stability is very likely the tendency to blame the self: to experience guilt as an individual and as a member of a class for failures that can also be attributed to economic and social institutions. A large proportion of the unemployed, the poor, and the women who find themselves in ill-paid, low status, deadend jobs feel that their unfortunate situation is deserved, that they are less intelligent, less industrious, and less meritorious than the affluent and the successful.

The prosperous are victims of the same form of displacement,

for they are also socialized to blame themselves, at least ambival-
ently, for the all too apparent pathologies of the society from
which they benefit. Like the disadvantaged, they act according to
the logic of their social situation; the incentive is strong to displace guilt onto a perception of character defects.

The targets of displaced resentments or guilt are often "catch-
all" enemies: people who become magnets for the suspicions and
anger of many different groups and therefore serve to condense
and transform a range of discontents and also to build political
coalitions, as noted earlier. The key factor that appears to make
people magnet targets is some characteristic that the majority in a
community has mutually defined as a symbol of suspect status:
ideology, skin color, religious belief, sometimes even failure to
keep one's lawn covered with grass or moving about an affluent
suburb on foot rather than by automobile. The most common
such characteristic doubtless is a nationality people have been
socialized to see as less human than the Americans, English, or
Swedes with whom they usually associate. Displacement of
resentments onto some peoples is easily orchestrated; for Rus-
sians, Salvadorans, Vietnamese, or Koreans as stereotypes are
condensations and transformations of other kinds of magnet
targets.

Cognitive Structuring through the Construction of Enemies

Both psychological theory and observations of everyday politics
suggest that every belief is systematically linked to others. Parts of
cognitive structures reinforce one another, imply one another,
and transform into one another. To see the liberal supporter of
gun control as an enemy of the good society is also to accept a
wider structure of beliefs: (1) Evil people, not social conditions
or class inequalities, create social problems; (2) We can solve the
problems raised by foreign enemies, domestic subversives, and
crime by shooting offenders; (3) Owners of guns will defend
democracy and property rights, not threaten them. Beliefs need
not be logically consistent, even if they are part of the same
cognitive structure; but each belief is influenced by the function it
plays in the wider set and presupposes the wider set.

Preoccupation with an enemy would seem to be a key facet of
many structures of beliefs that severely constrain political
thought and behavior. Such preoccupation keeps attention

focused upon a political world with a defined past, a destined future, a particular setting, and a prescribed set of relevant actions and actors with defined purposes. This constructed world makes it clear which policies are desirable and which are misconceived. The world in which Nazis were the enemy had a history of virulent anti-Semitism and an ominous future in which racial and religious prejudice was a critical danger, while enemies and allies were defined by their support and opposition to anti-Semitism. Jews are the enemy in a world in which they are responsible directly or indirectly for personal failures, disasters, wars, and economic troubles; and they constitute the key threat of defilement of racially pure peoples and of true religion and ethics. The enemy objectifies and symbolizes a constructed history, a setting, and a future state of affairs.

The set of beliefs that comprise such a cognitive structure systematically rearranges itself to maintain the focus upon an enemy when that claim is challenged; that it does so is a critical implication of the term "structure." Such rearrangement is readily accomplished, for there are always ambiguous terms, implicit connections, and substitutable assumptions that facilitate readjustment to counter logical or empirical challenges. If the "communists" Senator Joseph McCarthy alleged he had discovered in the army and the State Department cannot be found, their elusiveness proves their cleverness and deviousness. That homicide rates are substantially higher in countries that permit people to own guns than in those that do not becomes conclusive evidence of the ubiquity of crime in the first group and the greater need for citizens to protect themselves against criminals by acquiring guns. The cognitive structure that maintains belief in an enemy rests upon a presupposition or anxiety that is crucial to a self-conception and to continued pursuit of a political role.

Enemies are sometimes substituted for others to keep a cognitive structure credible and vital. As times change and fashions in naming threats change with them, enemies often succeed one another, though new enemies also coexist with the older ones. Since the Know Nothing movement of the 1830s definitions of the threatening alien in America have periodically shifted from Papists to anarchists to communists and, for a time, to fascists. In recent decades, third world terrorists have emerged as a new target, overlapping with communists. In the last century, liberals and radicals have defined their enemy as trusts, the FBI, the CIA, and multinational corporations, to name only the more prominent ones. Through American history potential or actual foreign enemies have succeeded one another: England, Mexico, Spain, Germany, Russia, North Korea, Cuba, Vietnam, Nicaragua. Regardless of whether a perception of threat is valid in any instance, enemies who are credible in the current time and situation are necessary components of the political system.

Antagonists also help to constitute subjectivity in politics. Politicized people define themselves in large part in terms of their opposition to other groups they fear and condemn. Leaders and aspirants to leadership are especially likely to build a persona on the basis of opposition to an enemy or a group of them. The phenomenon helps explain the attribution of enmity to people who, in the eyes of others, do no harm. It also helps explain the ubiquity and persistence of enemy construction in politics, for it is intimately linked to self-definition and to leadership.

A self-conception is a crucial element of any structure of cognitions because it establishes the moral perspective, the ideology, from which a person interprets the social world. To name specific enemies is to evoke specific ideologies. We know a great deal about the moral stance and the ideology of a person if we know his or her definition of the paramount political enemy: liberals, the police, the poor, the rich, the young, males, or Catholics.

The political uses of enemies are closely linked to the social groupings with which people identify. As linguistic and other cues induce people to define themselves as members of different groups, the perception of enemies changes acordingly. The identification of the self in national, religious, ethnic, ideological, economic, sexual, or other terms is the same process as the identification of enemies in those terms. Categorization, perception, and politics go hand in hand.

The world evoked by one enemy does not preclude preoccupation with other worlds and other enemies as well. To hate and fear blacks is no reason one cannot also fear and hate homosexuals, bankers, or dark skinned Asians. Sometimes these worlds are merged because the different enemies are perceived as allies or dupes of some one of them; sometimes they occupy separate mental compartments.

Opponents as Stabilizers

Long established enmities entail a highly predictable kind of discourse, as already noted, and a correspondingly predictable continuity in power, privileges, and relative resources. Hostile language and gestures that have lasted for a long time accordingly become signs of acquiescence in the continuation of the relationship while they continue in their banal forms. To stop exaggerating the enemy's dangerous potentialities or to employ physical force to eliminate him would signal change; but to continue verbal assaults and indecisive physical movements that have long taken place is to signal that all will remain as it has been: that the dramaturgy of enmity is consolidating public support for regimes, for causes, and for inequalities.

This phenomenon helps us understand the perpetuation for long periods of time, often for centuries, of exploitative relationships between social groups that blatantly violate the moral codes to which their adherents subscribe. Whites define their personal posture toward blacks as a caring one or as offering blacks the conditions in which they feel comfortable, even if the blacks are slaves, living in impoverished ghettos, or able to find only alienating work or no work at all.

Indeed, a moralistic discourse typically is central to the transaction between enemies: reaction formation complements rationalization. In consequence, unequal relationships become stabilized, each group learning its expected form of action and each episode in the sequence of hostilities rationalizing later ones and long-standing differences in material resources and privilege.

Sexuality and Attributions of Eroticism as Social Control

Repression of a group of people often entails attributing unique erotic qualities to the women of that group. The claim is common about black and Jewish women and about the women of rival ethnic groups. It appeared on a class basis in the *droit du Seigneur* and in later variations of the *droit* among plantation owners and among corporate executives.

Declarations that women of a feared group invite and enjoy sexual assault sometimes accompanies claims about their physical attractiveness. Especially blatant language of that kind circulated about black women in the postbellum American South; its social consequences there are revealing about its general political effect. The encouragement of assaults upon black women by white males in the culture of the South through the nineteenth and most of the twentieth century was a key buttress of black repression and exploitation, intimidating black men at least as radically as it degraded black women because the assaults amounted to a continuous demonstration of the men's powerlessness and subservience. Stories about the erotic qualities of classes of women must generally be understood as an integral aspect of group exploitation because they invent a difference that converts women into objects of aggression and at the same time serves as a sign of the degradation of the entire group.[5]

Sexuality is always political because it establishes bonds, strains, hostilities, and constraints and it generates symbols of the ideal and of the repugnant. The attribution of a unique measure of eroticism is blatantly political because it defines the group in terms that ignore individual characteristics and potentialities while highlighting a provocation to oppression.

Even a cursory review of the diverse psychological relationships that are central to politics highlights the role of libido in shaping them and changing them. There are personal bonds to leaders and to people who share in one's political actions and enthusiasms, but always with some ambivalence and often with deep ambivalence. The bond with enemies and with adversaries expresses both affection and hostility. The sadistic and masochistic gestures that abound in political maneuvers even more plainly resonate with sexual echoes. Judging others, flirting with their interests, paying court to superiors and degrading subordinates, celebrating political victories and grieving together after defeats—all these common political actions reveal sexual components. The conventional language that neatly separates the public from the private is very likely itself a reaction to the discomfort occasioned when it grows clear how intimately the personal and the political merge into one another.

A related and equally potent way in which sexuality permeates politics appears in the strong focus, in recent centuries, upon the

5. For American and European examples of this effect see: Gerda L. Lerner, *The Majority Finds Its Past* (New York: Oxford University Press, 1979), 71–73; George L. Mosse, *Nationalism and Sexuality* (New York: Howard Fertig, 1985), 133–52.

promotion of ideological conformity and the repression of dissent and rebellion through surveillance and control of people's bodies and through confessions of impermissible ideas and impulses in psychiatric interviews and in meetings under the aegis of the state.[6]

Bureaucratic Structures as Influences upon Enemy Construction

Some administrative organizations gain budgetary resources in the degree that a certain enemy is accepted as real and threatening. Staff members have an incentive to construct such enemies, for their careers, status, and income are at stake. Individuals who accept an ethos of suspicion are attracted to the organization in question as a place to work, and those who do not avoid making their careers in it. Peer pressures and self-interest can be counted on to reinforce the prevailing ideology, so that the organization's distinctive ethos is reinforced. It is no accident that the officials who rise to the top of the armed forces and the Pentagon are not doves, though some of these same officials become leading doves after they retire and so gain status from a new milieu and a different set of interests. Similarly, there are systematic reasons, stemming from the role relationships within the organization, that the top officials of the FBI, the CIA, and the legislative committees on the armed services and on internal security continue to identify enemies more zealously then the general population. To establish governmental agencies to deal with external or internal security is to guarantee that their top officials will see serious threats to security and so preserve a function, a budget, and careers. The point is not that officials invent threats that do not exist, but rather than security threats are usually ambiguous and that organizational functioning influences interpretations.

At the individual level the key psychological principle involved here is the link between motivation and perception, a link long recognized as significant.[7] The motivation is generated by

6. *Cf.* Michel Foucault, *The History of Sexuality.*

7. *Cf.* Julian E. Hochberg, "Psychophysics and Stereotype in Social Perception," in *Emerging Problems in Social Psychology* (Norman, Oklahoma: University Book Exchange, 1957), 117–41; Henri Tajfel, "Quantitative Judgment in Social Perception," *British Journal of Psychology* 50 (1959): 16–29; Jerome S. Bruner, "On Perceptual Readiness," *Psychological Review* 64 (1957): 123–52.

the creation of an organizational unit and the assignment of a particular function to it. While the conventional view holds that the establishment of such organizations is a response to existing threats and to popular fears of them, their creation is also a guarantee that the threats will continue to be taken as real and that the actions of hostile countries will make them self-fulfilling prophecies in some measure, for reasons considered earlier. Whether observers take the threat to be the reason for establishing the organization or the functioning organization to be the catalyst of the threat hinges on the breadth and depth of their historical perspective.

Some Consequences of Political Enemy Construction

The commonsense view that people perceive as enemies those who do or threaten harm manifestly does not describe their construction in politics. Many examples already cited demonstrate that the enemies who are targets of the most intense animus may threaten no harm at all.

The converse is also true: people who demonstrably hurt others severely are often not defined or perceived as enemies because their role in harassing others is not discernible, the facts are complex, or the source of harm is rationalized by ideology or symbolism. Public officials who adopt fiscal and monetary policies that throw millions of people out of work and impoverish a high proportion of them are seldom seen by their victims as enemies. Nor are corporate managers who pollute the environment in ways that bring lingering disease or early death to many people, especially if the pollution and the victimization are sufficiently widespread and slow rather than concentrated in a specific dump that brings discomfort, pain and disease to people whose plight is publicized.

In his chapter on "The Fetishism of Commodities" in volume 1 of *Capital,* Marx analyzes a paradigmatic instance of the displacement from public perception of people who are in a position to harm others. When we buy or sell commodities, he points out, we experience the transaction only as an exchange of objects, excluding from attention the social relations and power relations that are legitimized in the course of setting the price of a commodity, including the wages paid by entrepreneurs to the workers who produced it: "a . . . social relation between men . . . assumes, in their eyes, the fantastic form of a relation between things." The social relationship and the unequal power to inflict harm become invisible, a phenomenon that appears in other political interactions as well. Reification occurs with respect to both time and substance. Current troubles displace historical knowledge, and a focus upon commodities displaces awareness of exploitation.

Enemies, then, are identifiable persons or stereotypes of persons to whom evil traits, intentions, or actions can be attributed. It is not the harm that matters, but the attribution. A steep increase in unemployment is like a natural catastrophe or an act of God, with no personified enemy in sight. Blacks, Jews, or Vietnamese, by contrast, may symbolize satanic traits even if they cause no discernible harm. Enmity lies in the eye of the beholder. There may be evidence for it, or there may be none.

These examples suggest a related hypothesis about the basis of enemy construction. The domestic "enemies" who do no harm are often, though not always, low status, lower class, relatively powerless people, while those whose actions hurt others without bringing them an "enemy" label are likely to be high status, upper class, or relatively powerful. People who are the targets of prejudice and wield little power in the observable world are assumed to be enormously powerful and malevolent behind the scenes. So Jews are charged with controlling international banking or international communism or, as in the "Protocols of the Elders of Zion," with conspiring to control international politics.

The construction of domestic enemies reinforces established power relations in other ways as well. It fragments the population into hostile groupings and so minimizes the likelihood of a unified challenge to the power structure. Blacks, European ethnic groups, and native Americans are all disadvantaged, but expend energy resenting one another. Many middle class workers and business people resent welfare recipients. Adherents to far right and far left ideologies define one another as dangerous, and both groups are frequent targets of liberals. Many people see homosexuals or some religious groups as threats to the moral order. In short, divisions and hostilities moderate class divisions and so provide a kind of social cement.[8] While some one of these

8. *Cf.* David Truman, *The Governmental Process* (New York: Knopf, 1951), 159–69.

enmities occasionally erupts into violence, the cement usually prevents eruptions from escalating into revolutions even when they are serious, as in the labor and farm unrest of the thirties and in the ghetto riots and antiwar protests of the sixties.

Enemy construction typically grows from intellectual and emotional involvement in the rivalries, aspirations, and anxieties of the present, without attention to the changes over long time periods that explain contemporary conflicts and discontents. If it is mentioned at all, history becomes a set of myths to justify current resentments and aggressions rather than a basis for understanding and explanation. Within that ahistorical framework group actions and inactions are attributed to admirable or evil traits or to attitudes that rationalize definitions of enemies and allies.

An alternative view emerges when we look at the same phenomena in historical perspective, taking long term social and economic changes into account. It then appears that threatening behavior and physical attack, when they do occur, are a late stage of a train of psychological and political developments that have their origin in the conditions in which people live rather than in the psychological or cultural inadequacies of national, ethnic, racial, religious, sexual, or other groups.

The construction of enemies makes it psychologically and ethically possible to hurt or kill them, but everyday political language typically reverses the causal and time sequence, naming the enemy's inherent dangerousness as the cause of trouble, while masking displacement of grievances or guilt onto vulnerable targets. Such reversals of cause and consequence are endemic in political discourse when it justifies aggression and enemy construction. Communication about enemies, accordingly, exemplifies the performative nature of language in a striking way; this language is manifestly a form of action, not a tool for describing a situation.

The frightening implication is that anyone, no matter how well-intentioned, is likely to attribute harm to others when there is no warrant for doing so. The material situations of observers, the status differences, disadvantages, and privileges with which they live their lives and which confront them at a particular time, are crucial in shaping the perception of enemies. The belief that others are evil, even if it seems unwarranted to historians, is not to be understood as arbitrary, as accidental, or as a sign of inherent irrationality or immorality. In conducive social situations anyone can be defined as an enemy or categorize others that way for reasons that have nothing to do with the actions of the people who are labeled. Evil is banal because human beings are placed in situations in which many will predictably yield to the temptation to justify themselves by blaming others and, sometimes, to hurt, torture, or kill them. The state repeatedly reflects these impulses, harming human beings in the name of the people.

It is reassuring to assume that only in the exceptional case do people victimize others in order to make them scapegoats for social discontents. But the phenomenon is neither exceptional nor growing rare. It has been chronic in all lands and all eras and has been especially blatant in our own century: eighty-five years marked by two world wars; the holocaust; the systematic repression, torture, and killing of domestic political dissidents; genocide in many countries; and the quick succession of great power military operations of unprecedented destructiveness in third world regions, with all of these developments systematically linked to growing inequalities in wealth among and within nations.

To blame vulnerable groups for the sufferings and guilt people experience in their daily lives is emotionally gratifying and politically popular, and so the construction of enemies underlies not only domination, oppression, and war, but the policy formation, the elections, and the other seemingly rational and even liberal activities of the contemporary state as well.

5 *The Ambiguities of Political News*

It is chiefly news reports that stimulate the construction of political spectacles. Those involved in making, reporting, and editing news accordingly have an incentive to shape it so as to attract audiences and, sometimes, to encourage particular interpretations through its content and form. Interest groups, public officials, and editorial staffs share an interest in making news dramatic; economic, psychological, and ideological concerns reinforce each other in this respect. Dramatization, simplification, and personification (including the personification of historical trends and social institutions into leaders and enemies) are common means, especially in lead sentences and headlines.

Other devices abet these in making news accounts "hyperreal" for those people who have some reason to pay attention to them. A common one is the contriving of "pseudoevents" so that they will be reported and create specific beliefs.[1] A closely related tactic is the depiction of events to evoke assumptions about the past, the future, and agents who bring about good or evil outcomes. Such narratives, giving developments in the news a particular meaning, need not be spelled out. They may be more effective as propaganda if they remain implicit and so less likely to be rebutted: references to "workfare," for example, that call up a story about the laziness of welfare recipients in the past and the wholesome role of coercion in making them more responsible.

Narratives are likely to be ideologically diverse because they reflect the interests of disparate constituents. The FBI and the American Civil Liberties Union both generate stories about the origins and outcomes of threats to law and to human rights, but the stories emerging from these organizations teach conflicting lessons. Different institutions similarly disseminate alternative beliefs about which behaviors are deviant and which acceptable. In these ways narratives, political interests, and the social situ-

---

1. See Daniel Boorstin, *The Image: A Guide to Pseudo-Events in America* (New York: Atheneum, 1971).

ations of audiences interact with one another to construct, and sometimes resolve, issues dramaturgically.

Such characteristics of news accounts imbue them with two politically crucial properties: ambiguity and a capacity for interesting some people and boring others, making it easier for audiences to project meanings into the news that reinforce their prior beliefs. If news stories challenge deeply held assumptions, they can be ignored; and if they point in no clear direction, they can be interpreted to conform to prior assumptions.

Social problems, leaders, enemies, and other recurring themes in political news display the curious property that each reference is typically unambiguous for an individual for the moment, while the connotations of each reference vary widely among individuals, groups, and situations. A political news item is therefore likely to give each reader, viewer, or auditor the impression of a specific meaning that belies its utility as a catalyst for other ideological projections. This phenomenon facilitates tactical game playing by all who try to influence outcomes, and it makes for uncertainty in planning and evaluating political strategies.

This chapter considers the contributions to ambiguity in political news from some related social phenomena: the conventions of news reporting, the efforts of interest groups to shape what is reported, disparate social conditions, dubious philosophical assumptions about the nature of reality, dominant ideology, and some psychological processes. All of these influence news interpretation substantially, but not in the same way in diverse situations or for different people.

What News Matters?

The media decide what is worth reporting. Some people and organizations are accepted as "news sources," and some kinds of events are assumed to be pregnant with meaning for the general public. There is, in short, a stylized view of what constitutes news: a view that insures the dissemination of many items that have little bearing on future developments or on the quality of life and that preclude dissemination of other stories that have a vital bearing on both. A statement by or about a chief of state or high government official is news regardless of its importance or its validity. Such items underline the status of the official in question and sometimes have little other bearing on the lives of their auditors and viewers. Similarly, some events, such as elections, are defined as news worth reporting regardless of whether they bring significant consequences for anyone. By contrast, a technical action by a central bank or defense ministry that can mean prosperity or disaster, life or death, for thousands of people may not even be mentioned in most newspapers or broadcasts. Nor is there any assurance that the long-term effects of public policies will ever be reported as news, though they are the crucial test of the effectiveness of policies. They typically cannot be known until long after the policy has been established, and they are often complex and not easily reported in journalistic language. Political news accordingly highlights conflicts in elections, legislative bodies, administrative agencies, courts, and elsewhere while paying little or no attention to whether the victories and defeats in these arenas have made a difference in people's lives and, if so, what kind of difference. This tendency is strengthened, and perhaps generated, by the fascination of both liberals and conservatives with political processes and their distaste for examining outcomes that highlight inequities and inequalities in the results of the processes.

There is, then, no necessary link between the importance of a development for well-being and its prominence in print or electronic news. Many items that the media feature are important. The point, however, is that importance (by whatever test) is not the criterion by which they are chosen. It is evident that conventions about what should be reported and what ignored become indicators for many people of what events are to be taken as significant regardless of some skepticism. A free press, competing news media, and alert and competent news staffs are therefore no guarantee that the public can act effectively in pursuit of its interests.

Contrasts and Oppositions

Every news item takes its meaning from the context of other news in which it appears and from the background assumptions of its audiences. Because both the context and the background assumptions vary among spectators and among the situations in which they find themselves, the same news item may carry a wide range of meanings. An account of hunger, homelessness, or suffering holds a different meaning during a recession than it does in the course of an economic boom and different meanings as well according to how sensitive observers are to the plight of others. The same point applies to news of business failures, bankruptcies, and record profits.

In other ways as well implicit comparisons and contrasts furnish benchmarks that shape the meanings of political news. If the highlighted item on any day is an account of a presidential vacation, it means chiefly that nothing more important or disturbing has occurred recently. There is no way to gauge the significance of a verbal attack on an opposition leader, foreign or domestic, until one knows whether the denunciation is part of a history of alternating escalation and détente in the relationship, a response to a similar statement, or a change from friendship to hostility.

The source of a news item and its intended audience similarly mold its significance. A report that a member of the John Birch Society has labeled a policy subversive has a different meaning from news that a liberal has done so. Similarly, a politician who criticizes a labor bill in a speech to the National Association of Manufacturers makes a different statement than when he or she uses the same words to the AFL-CIO.

The spectacle, in short, carries no meaning in itself. It is always a gloss on the phenomenal worlds of individuals and groups. The pertinent qualities of the phenomenal world include its history, its setting, its agents of good and evil, its definitions of some people as irrelevant, and the range of potentialities it promises for the future. In all these respects people's worlds differ, though shared material conditions provide substantial overlaps. Because experiences and imaginations are complex, every individual inhabits contradictory social worlds in some degree. The same people who see American military interventions in the third world as dangerous to peace and as repressive of the poor may also see them as defenses against communist aggression. News stories catalyze scenarios that are remote from everyday life but take their configurations and their significance from the experiences of everyday life. In every sense, then, their meanings are relative. The more thoroughly dialectical their analysis, the more fully their meanings reveal themselves. Analysis becomes adequate in the measure that it encompasses the multivalence of which the mind is capable.

News, then, is not so much a description of events as a catalyst of political support and opposition in the light of the spectator's sensitivities, areas of ignorance, and ideological stance. The acceptance of a story plot that defines the background of a reported development and its future consequences is crucial. The scenarios for the future that news accounts evoke are rarely acted out according to their scripts. They are aborted or replaced by alternative scenarios implicit in later news accounts, but before that happens they influence political support and action. In this light, politics consists of a panoply of overlapping and conflicting spectacles that fade from the scene as they give birth to their successors.

There are separate spectacles for different groups of people. Some see some one issue as so important that it colors everything else. Is a development good for gunowners, Cuban exiles, Catholics, the handicapped? Diverse enthusiasms and fears define attention to news stories or obliviousness to them: degree of interest in sports, or South African apartheid, or ecumenism, or water rights in the West, or zoning a local neighborhood. Spectacles focused on parochial issues or particular concerns coexist, with little connection between them and no necessary effect upon each other. They are news for some and of little interest to most. Any concern at all can be counted on to elicit news accounts if it is broad and strong enough to entail economic or psychological benefits for political interest groups or for the media. In this sense a news catalyst is available for every shared concern. The spectacles of politics change readily and so do their consequences for arousal or quiescence.

News of controversial issues keeps tensions between groups alive or intensifies them or broadens them. An account of a court decision on abortion carries conflicting connotations for feminists and for opponents of abortion; every such story buttresses the antagonism between the two groups.

The Interpretation of News Stories

The commonsensical view of the news is essentially the same as the positivist view. The world of newsworthy events is distinct from the people who report it and learn about it. Reporting should be objective, though the ideal is not always achieved; so political developments are the same for everyone, though some people pay more attention to them than others, and some misinterpret them.

If the meaning of the news lay only in the "objective" physical movements of people, currency, bombs, welfare checks, and so on, this model of the physical world would make some sense. But the premise is plainly absurd. It is only the meanings people attribute to observations, not sense perceptions or discernible physical movements in themselves, that make them important or irrelevant. And the significance of a troop invasion, a cut in the discount rate or in tax rates, or an electoral ballot count is always ambiguous and usually controversial. It is the ambiguity and the controversy that make developments political in character. So there can be no world of events distinct from the interpretations of observers.

Though there are separate spectacles, the number is limited, for a spectacle is a social phenomenon, not an individual idiosyncrasy. Its meanings spring from common definitions of problems, prospects, and policies; idiosyncratic beliefs and dreams carry no political importance unless they come to be publicly supported or opposed by others. At any time, then, the number of issues comprising the range of extant spectacles is not likely to be large. From this point of view exposure to the news is part of a process of self-definition as well as definition of the world, helping catalyze the emergence of each individual as a loyal follower, an outraged patriot, a rebel against oppressive authority, a proud Republican, and so on.

Interpretation pervades every phase of news creation and dissemination. Officials, interest groups, and critics anticipate the interpretations of particular audiences, shaping their acts and language so as to elicit a desired response. The audiences for news are the ultimate interpreters, paying attention to some stories, ignoring most, and fitting news accounts into a story plot that reflects their respective values. For any audience, then, an account is an interpretation of an interpretation. An adequate analysis would see it as a moment in a complex chain of interpretations, each phase of the process anticipating later interpretations and helping to shape them. Ambiguity and subjectivity are neither deviations nor pathologies in news dissemination; they constitute the political world. To posit a universe of objective events is a form of mysticism that legitimizes the status quo because the interpretation that is defined as objective is likely to reflect the dominant values of the time.

The expectations raised by news reports may become self-fulfilling prophecies. Reports of a shortage of any commodity encourage hoarding, more severe shortages, and price increases. Reports that a foreign country or a domestic group is about to take hostile action can encourage provocations that catalyze hostilities. But such expectations may never be realized: developments that surprise everyone also occur frequently.

The spectacle, in short, is a partly illusory parade of threats and reassurances, most of which have little bearing upon the successes and ordeals people encounter in their everyday lives, and some of which create problems that would not otherwise occur. The political spectacle does not promote accurate expectations or understanding, but rather evokes a drama that objectifies hopes and fears.

Government officials are both actors in the spectacle and an audience for it, though it is easier to recognize the former role than the latter. Like other spectators, they interpret news of public affairs in the light of their social situations and ideologies, doubtless with an especially strong commitment to the constructions that justify their official actions. That they can influence what is reported is no reason they need be skeptical about its skewing. On the contrary, their involvement provides a strong incentive to rationalize the official account; officials who interact also reinforce the rationalization for one another. As a result, the same interpretation can dominate policy making indefinitely even if there is the clearest evidence that its premises are dubious or invalid. American policy in Vietnam in the 1960s illustrates the point, as do many other foreign and domestic policy failures. In such cases, widely reported criticism of official policy increases the defensiveness of policy makers and their obliviousness to inconsistent facts.[2]

The influence upon public policy of people who forge a shared definition of reality exemplifies George Herbert Mead's view that the formation of mind, of the self, and of social action

---

2. *Cf.* Irving L. Janis, *Groupthink: Psychological Studies of Policy Decisions and Fiascoes* (Boston: Houghton Mifflin, 1982).

all involve the social psychological process of taking the role of the "significant other" (which may be a "generalized other"). But to recognize that phenomenon is to reject the pluralist premise that contending groups have an equitable chance to influence policy. Some like-minded groups control the resources to allocate valued benefits while others interact with one another socially and symbolically to insure docile acceptance of their deprivations. The powerful and the powerless cooperate in this way to solidify each other's positions; symbolic interactions complement economic and social disparities.

News and Powerlessness

Audience interpretations of the spectacle are manifestly constrained in some measure by what is reported, what is omitted and, perhaps most fundamentally, by the implications in news reports respecting limits upon the ability of citizens to influence policy. In subtle ways the public is constantly reminded that its role is minor, largely passive, and at most reactive. The intense publicity given to voting and elections is itself a potent signal of the essential powerlessness of political spectators because elections are implicitly a message about the *limits* of power. Everyone who grows up in our society is bound to become aware, at some level of consciousness, that an individual vote is more nearly a form of self-expression and of legitimation than of influence and that the link between elections and value allocations is tenuous. The reiteration in patriotic oratory and grade school civics lessons that the people control the government comes to be recognized as a way of insuring support for governmental actions people dislike and over which they exercise no effective control.

The limited power of the public is implicit in most language about policy formation in a still more potent way: its depiction of policy formation as taking place in a forum that is remote from everyday life. Stories evoking the high status of officials, their intricate negotiations with one another, their unique access to intelligence, and the privileges their offices confer on them are at the same time narratives about the exclusion of the rest of the population from that special world. In this respect the political spectacle evokes something like the awe and sense of personal powerlessness characteristic of a religious posture; an implicit association with the religious attitude doubtless underlies this kind of political language. Like religious myths about great events in a time and place outside everyday experience, these political accounts build an intensified appeal and an acquiescent response upon their remoteness.[3]

Political developments justifying the widespread acceptance of sacrifices similarly evoke a remote power or place. They may refer to a foreign "power" that is acting aggressively, while the same kinds of stories in the foreign country keep a sense of vulnerability and dread alive there. Inflation and unemployment are similarly reported as happenings outside the control of the people who lose their jobs and have to pay higher prices. Crime, economic recession, mental illness, and other social problems are often treated as fated events as well. Accounts can emphasize or minimize a sense of inevitability and impotence according to whether they treat structures as untouchable or as constructed.

The dissemination of contradictory messages and the alternation of threat and reassurance, of emphasis upon escalation and stories of détente, serve both to keep people anxious and to keep them docile. Inconsistency is the natural response of regimes to the concurrent pressures upon them and so requires no scheming, no deliberate effort to minimize criticism or maximize acquiescence. Yet it achieves these effects splendidly.

A set of frequently used terms also helps induce an acquiescent posture toward the acts of public officials. Words like "public," "official," "due process of law," "the public interest," and "the national interest" have no specific referent, but induce a considerable measure of acceptance of actions that might otherwise be viewed with skepticism or hostility. Such terms evoke a sacred aura, as do inaugurations, flags, imposing buildings, and judicial robes. These symbols help erase the sense of guilt, humiliation, or injustice that acquiescence would create if public officials were seen as ordinary people conferring valuable benefits on some and imposing severe sacrifices on others.

Related language forms encourage public support for especially severe penalties against people who resist authority. From "contempt of court" through "resisting an officer" to the names of specific crimes the public is exposed to terms justifying punish-

3. *Cf.* Mircea Eliade, *The Sacred and the Profane* (New York: Harcourt Brace, 1957), 20–67.

ments that, in a context free from the symbolism of "reasons of state," might be viewed in the light of such alternative symbols as "freedom of expression" and "human rights." Diverse language games construct alternative political worlds, with radically different notions of fairness. In an important sense each game excludes other possibilities, and both the contrasting examples just noted divert attention from the role played in governmental actions by class and ideological interests. These examples make it clear that the terms news stories routinely deploy mean a great deal more than they denote.

Human Interest Stories

As suggested earlier, news accounts largely ignore everyday life, drawing an artificial boundary between the events people confront directly and those that are reported to them and treating the latter as the more significant. But an examination of the *effects* of public policies requires a focus upon everyday life because it is in the conditions of people's lives that economic, social, and political actions exert their effects.

As if to paper over their inattention to daily life, the media devote considerable attention to one kind of public event that they present as a private one: the human interest story. It is public in the sense that it deals either with the private life of a celebrity or with a kind of pathetic, heroic, or scandalous action that carries instant and wide appeal regardless of who does it.

Human interest stories are political events because they reinforce the view that individual action is crucial: that biography is the paramount component of historical accounts. A focus upon the "private" lives of celebrities underlines their significance as public figures. Stories about the heroic actions of ordinary people and the disasters from which they suffer similarly erase structural conditions from notice, even while they divert attention from the rest of the political spectacle. Heroic, pathetic, and prurient stories sell papers, build Nielsen ratings, and help prevent more revealing news from disturbing ideologies.

Types of News and Their Constructed Meanings

Newspapers and news broadcasts offer a mélange of disparate stories, varying in content, in form, and in the associations they evoke. But because their meanings depend upon the ideologies of their audiences, there is an intriguing sense in which they reinforce the world view of the auditor or reader regardless of their content.

All news calls for interpretation in the light of political considerations. Even "acts of God," the class of news events that occur regardless of human planning or action, are political because earthquakes, storms, floods, shipwrecks, crop failures, and other instances of the genre raise questions about who was responsible for efforts to minimize damage and help victims, whether these measures were adequate, whether the event exerted differential effects on the poor, on business enterprises, and so on. There are likely to be claims of profiteering, looting, and other actions that define some as villains and others as victims or as heroes. In an even more apparent way, news of events brought about by human intention becomes the occasion for beliefs about origins and consequences that reflect and reinforce ideology. Threats from foreign governments or "terrorists," elections, crimes, welfare policy, and economic trends involve pervasive ambiguities that people resolve in ways that reflect their class, gender, national, ethnic, and other identifications.[4]

In a crucial sense, then, the specific content of news items is often irrelevant so far as their influence upon political support and opposition is concerned. No matter what happens or how it is reported, a large proportion of the public will interpret it so as to reinforce their current predilections regarding issues, parties, leaders, enemies, and social problems. That a war does or does not break out in the Middle East or in Central America, that candidate A or party B won an election, that an earthquake ravaged an Italian province, that prices are rising or falling, that a president was assassinated[5] seems to make little difference so far as long-term definitions of the worlds people inhabit are concerned, for there are always aspects of the spectacle to capture attention and transform reported news into an experienced world that rationalizes actions, fears, and aspirations. It is the dynamism of the spectacle and its ambiguity, not its substance, that are politically and psychologically critical. To inhabitants of the region

4. See chapter 4 for an extended analysis of this phenomenon.
5. *Cf.* Murray Edelman and Rita James Simon, "Presidential Assassinations: Their Meaning and Impact on American Society," *Ethics* 79 (April 1969): 199–221.

hit by the earthquake and to the family and cabinet of the assassinated president the events in question are immediate experiences as well as spectacle. But to newspaper readers in Tokyo and television watchers in New York these items are pictures in the mind that mean what they need to mean to help them justify their lives. News reports divert attention from immediate experience and help focus it upon a constructed reality.

Experienced worlds sometimes change radically and with them the meanings attributed to news accounts. Radically altered material or cultural conditions bring new phenomena: better or worse economic outlooks; a new prospect of scientific and material progress, as in the latter part of the nineteenth century in the western world; the changed outlook that accompanied the great migrations from Europe to America in the nineteenth and early twentieth centuries and the mass migration of American blacks to the north in the 1950s. Such major changes in definition of the social world and in self-definition underline the distinction between felt experiences and those that flow from news reports of events one never touches. Language mediates both, but with different constraints.

The Construction of News Appeal

Some news reports haunt consciousness, while others are easily ignored, discounted, or forgotten. News of the unexpected and of personalities is more likely to be noticed and remembered than are historical or economic accounts that help explain the unexpected or that depict conspicuous personalities (whether leaders, enemies, or victims) as agents or pawns of more fundamental events. Both the unexpected happening and the conspicuous personality, then, depend for part of their psychological appeal upon the isolation of events and actions from whatever makes them understandable, whatever would minimize surprise and mystery. The event without a history calls upon spectators to provide it with one, and with a future as well, a psychological process that encourages the evocation of a social world that reflects personal anxieties and expectations and therefore carries a strong appeal, though not necessarily a pleasant one. To explain entails attention to patterns in past events that make current ones more understandable and so less surprising, a process that narrows the appeal of an account and defines it as scholarship rather than news.

A great deal of routine political news deals with governmental procedures that guarantee a contest; people take sides and so create suspense respecting an outcome. Elections, legislative battles, court cases, "summit" meetings, treaty negotiations, and other competitive events are opportunities for the news media to focus upon situations that involve both some element of surprise and personalities who win or lose. That they recur and comprise a high proportion of reported news guarantees that there will be systematic displacement of explanatory accounts and systematic distortion of the meanings of developments, for the influence of these institutionalized contests upon well-being is typically both dubious and exaggerated.

There is a kind of Gresham's law of news prominence: dramatic incidents involving individuals in the limelight displace attention from the larger configurations that explain the incidents and much else as well. Whether a politician unethically leaked a story exposing the failure of a policy becomes more important than whether the story is accurate. Who favors and opposes a proposal and what tactics they deploy displaces attention from its consequences for well-being. The experienced political world hinges on what interest groups can induce the media to report and what experiences those reports displace. In every case a widening of the frame (in time, space, logic, and empirical links) within which an event is viewed would change its meaning but would also create an account typically categorized as research rather than as news and often as dull rather than dramatic.

The ingenuity of the human mind in constructing worlds and the capacity of language to indulge that talent are subtle and concealed, but they are also the fundamental influences upon politics.

6 Political Language and Political Reality

Throughout this account of spectacle construction, language has been a prominent actor. Metaphors, other tropes, and ambiguity encourage people in disparate social situations to define themselves, others, and the conditions of their lives through a spectacle that normally rationalizes those conditions. This chapter offers a wider perspective on the role of language in helping to evoke political realities.

The most incisive twentieth-century students of language converge from different premises on the conclusion that language is the key creator of the social worlds people experience, not a tool for describing an objective reality. The "linguistic turn" in philosophy, social psychology, and literary theory has called attention to language games that construct alternative realities, grammars that transform the perceptible into nonobvious meanings, and language as a form of action that generates radiating chains of connotations while undermining its own assumptions and assertions.

The theorists who have explored the general links among language, action and thought have analysed the various senses in which language use is an aspect of creativity;[1] but those who focus upon specifically political language are chiefly concerned with its capacity to reflect ideology, mystify, and distort, which is one kind of creativity.[2] The more perspicacious of them deny that an undistorting language is possible in a social world marked by inequalities in resources and status, though the notion of an undistorted language may be useful as an evocation of an ideal benchmark.

The critical element in political maneuver for advantage is the

1. I mean especially Ludwig Wittgenstein, Noam Chomsky, Jacques Derrida, Michel Foucault, and those parts of Jürgen Habermas's work that deal with "emancipatory" communication.
2. The emphasis upon political language as distorting or mystifying is a key theme in the work of Harold Lasswell, George Orwell, Jürgen Habermas, Charles Osgood, Jacques Ellul, Hans Magnus Enzensberger, Lance Bennett, and Michael Shapiro.

103

creation of meaning: the construction of beliefs about events, policies, leaders, problems, and crises that rationalize or challenge existing inequalities. The strategic need is to immobilize opposition and mobilize support. While coercion and intimidation help to check resistance in all political systems, the key tactic must always be the evocation of interpretations that legitimize favored courses of action and threaten or reassure people so as to encourage them to be supportive or to remain quiescent. Allocations of benefits must themselves be infused with meanings: whose well-being does a policy threaten and whose does it enhance?

It is language about political events, not the events in any other sense, that people experience; even developments that are close by take their meaning from the language that depicts them. So political language *is* political reality; there is no other so far as the meaning of events to actors and spectators is concerned.

But that statement poses the problem rather than resolving it for it challenges us to examine the complex link between language and meaning. Every sentence is ambiguous. Dictionaries cannot tell us what language means; the social situations and the concerns of human beings who think and act define meanings. An increase in the defense budget signifies security for some and insecurity for others. The same is true of gun control, capital punishment, and most other governmental actions. Wider eligibility for welfare benefits means encouragement of laziness and incompetence to many, and it means the safeguarding of lives and dignity to many others. An action typically carries different meanings in different situations. Language about politics is a clue to the speaker's view of reality at the time, just as an audience's interpretation of the same language is a clue to what may be a different reality for them. If there are no conflicts over meaning, the issue is not political, by definition.

Political developments and the language that describes them are ambiguous because the aspects of events, leaders, and policies that most decisively affect current and future well-being are uncertain, unknowable, and the focus of disputed claims and competing symbols. Even when there is consensus about what observably happened or was said, there are conflicting assumptions about the causes of events, the motives of officials and interest groups, and the consequences of courses of action. So it is not what can be seen that shapes political action and support, but what must be supposed, assumed, or constructed. Do foreign troops in a troubled area encourage peace or more intensive fighting? Is Ronald Reagan a well-meaning and effective leader who represents the common people's aspirations against elitist liberals and intellectuals, or is he an articulate front for mean-spirited corporate executives and a menace to the poor?

There is no way to establish the validity of any of these positions to the satisfaction of those who have a material or moral reason to hold a different view. Reason and rationalization are intertwined. That intertwining and the impossibility of marshalling evidence that is persuasive to everyone are the hallmarks of political argument; they are not the occasional or the regrettable exceptional case. Ambiguity, contradiction, and evocations that reflect material situations are central and pervasive.

In short, it is not "reality" in any testable or observable sense that matters in shaping political consciousness and behavior, but rather the beliefs that language helps evoke about the causes of discontents and satisfactions, about policies that will bring about a future closer to the heart's desire, and about other unobservables. Their social situations make people sensitive to some political news, promises, and threats and insensitive to other communications.

Language is only one facet of the situation, but a critical one: the aspect that most directly interprets developments by fitting them into a narrative account providing a meaning for the past, the present, and the future compatible with an audience's ideology. Such accounts are vulnerable to criticism; but they succeed repeatedly in suspending disbelief, in retaining political support, or in marshalling opposition regardless of consequences that might call the accounts into question. Military interventions in the third world that bolster corrupt oligarchies and stifle peasant demands, for example, have been rationalized for many years on the ground that they support democracy by preventing a communist takeover engineered in Moscow or Havana. Neither experience nor repeated failures to bring democracy or peace diminish the potency of linguistic accounts that mesh with anticommunist ideology or, in other societies, with communist ideology.

The language that generates and reinforces beliefs about who are allies and who are enemies is an especially striking instance of the projection of divergent assumptions into words and sentences. Language often evokes a belief that particular groups are evil or harmful even when the language of history, analysis, and science suggests that they are scapegoats rather than enemies. Jews under the Third Reich, accused heretics under the Inquisition, liberals in the fifties, and countless other victims of discrimination testify to the power of language in particular situations to evoke a political world in which persecution is justified, even while the same words signify gross injustice to people in other situations.

Because most political news and debate is irrelevant to the quality of people's lives, it detracts from their ability to pursue their own interests effectively. We are inundated with accounts of election campaigns, legislative debates, and the statements of high officials, but none of these means anything at all for how well people live until they are implemented; and the forms of eventual implementation, or whether it will occur at all, cannot be known from the publicized language.

The spectacle that political language constructs is dynamic: concerned with problems, crises, challenges, and differences of opinion over how to deal with them; with new laws and new executive actions and high court decisions. It bemuses people's minds and places them in a social world marked by constant threats and constant reassurances. But the continuous bombardment of news about a changing political spectacle contrasts sharply with the static pattern of value allocations: the persistence of class, racial, gender, national, and other inequalities in resources, status, and hardships regardless of short-run fluctuations or news about political actions. For the observer of politics who focuses upon historical change rather than the kaleidoscope of publicized events, there is far less in the most widely publicized political language than meets the ear or the eye. While most political language marks little change in how well people live, it has a great deal to do with the legitimation of regimes and the acquiescence of people in actions they had no part in initiating.

Language consists of sound waves or of marks on paper that become meaningful because people project some significance into them, not because of anything inherent in the sounds or the marks. It takes on meaning and enables human beings to think symbolically because it is social in character. We make something of phonemes, grammar, and syntax by contemplating them for the perspectives of other people who are important to us. In George Herbert Mead's formulation this is taking the role of the significant other.[3] In Lev Vygotsky's formulation it is using "inner speech": an imagined conversation with others that also constitutes "thought."[4] Meaning springs from interactions with others, not from inside an isolated individual's head. Even if Noam Chomsky is right in his conjecture that human beings are genetically endowed with a universal grammar, the *content* of propositions is socially structured and constructed, as Chomsky recognizes. It follows that the economic and social conditions in which people find themselves are decisive influences upon their interpretations of language, and especially of political language. The transformation of situations into meanings is a complex process and plainly takes different forms, ranging from simple expression of class, gender, or other interests to rationalizations of disadvantages or privileges. Both the disadvantaged who passively accept their lot because they experience the world as a place where people get what they deserve and the rebels who struggle against a world in which they experience injustice as rampant illustrate the intimate link between social conditions and meaning construction.

Perhaps the central intellectual obstacle to recognition of language as a facet of the social situation and no more is our language about language: our categorization of it as a separate entity, as something distinct from interaction with others. Such reification of a perspective as a separate entity encourages the attribution of independent power and independent existence to words and sentences, with the result that observation, analysis, and interpretation are aborted.

If the thesis that language is a key bulwark of established institutions is valid, then the language we conventionally label nonpolitical should also serve that function. The language of the helping professions functions as a form of political action.[5] The

---

3. George Herbert Mead, *Mind, Self, and Society* (Chicago: University of Chicago Press, 1934).

4. Lev Vygotsky, *Thought and Language* (Cambridge: MIT Press, 1962).

5. Murray Edelman, *Political Language* (New York: Academic Press, 1977), chap. 4.

language of social science does so as well, especially when it purports to be nonpolitical and objective. A reader of the American politics textbooks and journals finds in them a great deal of attention to elections, rational choice, leadership, participation, and regulation: i.e., to the reassuring procedures, and little attention to the inequalities, forms of social control, and social pathologies that are often the outcomes of the procedures. The language that purges consciousness of the disturbing consequences of established institutions is defined and ordinarily accepted as objective and scientific, while language that calls attention to such consequences is defined and ordinarily accepted as ideological and polemical. Clearly, the terms "objective," "ideology," and "polemical" as used in academic writing and speech are themselves political.

Because the potency of political language does not stem from its descriptions of a "real" world but rather from its reconstructions of the past and its evocation of unobservables in the present and of potentialities in the future, language usage is strategic. It is always part of a course of action to enable people to live with themselves and with what they do and to marshall support for causes.

It is instructive to consider in just what sense Harold Lasswell's celebrated statement that, "Politics is the process by which the irrational bases of society are brought out into the open,"[6] holds true. People manifestly *can* choose among alternative courses of action to make desired outcomes somewhat more likely; but there are profound differences among forms of activity in how fully such rationality can be achieved. When objectives are comparatively noncontroversial and inequalities in resources and well-being are not integrally linked to value differences and to self conceptions, the fitting of means to ends is easiest and the term "rationality" makes some sense. In the natural sciences, the arts, and pragmatic everyday activities those who find ways to achieve generally supported ends are recognized and supported, though there is often some controversy over the success of some efforts.

In politics the situation is fundamentally different, and the very notion of rationality may be inappropriate, whether it is

6. Harold Lasswell, *Psychopathology and Politics* (Chicago: University of Chicago Press, 1930).

defined in terms of logical and effective means or in terms of substantive achievement of goals. Means and ends are integrally connected in such a way that it is never clear which is which, so that the terms themselves become political weapons. Are capital punishment, abortion, nuclear warfare or tax increases means to achieve a desirable goal or evils in themselves? What about welfare payments, governmental subsidies to industry, regulation of industry, and protection of the rights to speak and act in ways that offend some?

In politics, moreover, the incentive to preserve privileges or to end inequalities is always crucial, offering fertile psychological ground for using language and action strategically, including slippery definitions of means, ends, costs, benefits, and rationality. In some measure these problems with the language of rational choice doubtless apply in all fields; but in political maneuver they are so severe and so central that the issue is transformed, encouraging irrationality and ideology in the name of reason.

The reasons people offer for their political actions and preferences are also rationalizations, then, as Freud recognized. To make the distinction is itself a strategy, whether or not it is self-conscious. The human mind readily rationalizes any political position in a way that will be persuasive for an audience that wants to be convinced. That is what political discussion mainly consists of. The cogency and the appeal of a political argument depend far more on how sensitively it rationalizes the social situation of its audience than on any inherent rationality in its language, for rationality is itself a construction.

A popular school of thought holds that encouragement to give "good reasons" for political preferences assures at least a modicum of rationality in political choice.[7] The lesson of history is clear, unfortunately, that good reasons have been offered for every course of political action ever undertaken, that they have indeed often won wide public support, but that the consequences have all too often been experienced as disastrous, immoral, or the fruit of inexcusable stupidity. "Good reasons," like all political language, can be strategically effective, but they cannot assure a rational choice if, indeed, that term itself has any meaning other than a strategic or rationalizing one. How good a reason is

7. Bryan Barry, *Political Argument* (New York: Humanities Press, 1966).

depends upon its premise; but in politics the premise is typically controversial and not susceptible of verification, as already noted.

Habermas offers a thoughtful variation of the "good reasons" position that takes account of a critical pitfall: the constraints that hierarchical differences in status, authority, or other means of influence and coercion impose upon discourse. In Habermas's "ideal speech situation" there are no such differences and hence no constraints.[8] He believes, moreover, that people can in some measure presuppose the ideal speech situation even when it does not exist because the very use of language presupposes it. Perhaps an individual can occasionally achieve that kind of emancipation from social constraints, but the historical record is clear that group discussion and governmental policy formation do not achieve it. The Habermasian ideal speech situation offers an optimistic view, that may be warranted, of how discourse might become emancipatory in a society without capitalism or governmental or corporate or military hierarchies; but it provides little hope that political language in the world we inhabit can become something more than a sequence of strategies and rationalizations. The Supreme Court has justified the preventive detention of children in prison as a form of therapy for the children,[9] and the President has called the MX missile a "peacekeeper" even while conceding that it has little military use. These arguments and countless others like them in all countries and all eras have proven persuasive to large numbers of people because they reflect their fears or their hopes while others regard them as the epitome of false logic and immorality. What is accepted as a "good reason" need not tell much about the cogency of its argument but *is* a sensitive index to the problems, aspirations, and social situation of its audience. Although individuals manifestly can act morally and can judge others' behavior, the language of politics serves often to rationalize actions that violate the moral codes of the community and of the actors themselves.

But problems, aspirations, and social conditions are also subject to interpretation; they are constructions of language as well. It begins to grow clear that political language, like all texts,

8. Jürgen Habermas, "Toward a Theory of Communicative Competence," *Inquiry*, 13 (1970): 360–75; "A Postscript to Knowledge and Human Interests," *Philosophy of the Social Sciences*, 3 (1973): 157–85.
9. Schall v. Martin, 81 L. Ed. 2d. 207 (1984).

Political Language and Political Reality 111

can be understood as creating an endless chain of ambiguous associations and constructions that offer wide potentialities for interpretation and for manipulation.

It should follow that people in the same social situations use similar language to cope with the problems they face, and that kind of predictability is characteristic of a great deal of political language. Most of it is banal, precisely because it reassures speaker and audience that whatever they think will serve their interests is justifiable. The language in which heads of states justify larger arms budgets, police chiefs justify restrictions on the procedural rights of suspects, agriculture secretaries justify protections of the income of agribusiness enterprises, or liberals justify regulation of business to protect consumers is highly stylized and predictable most of the time, though its users may experience it as the epitome of creative and rational argument. The exchange of claims and assertions that have been made in similar situations many times before is the classic obbligato that accompanies the political spectacle, and, as George Orwell suggested in making a similar point, it has the same lulling effect on the mental faculties as responsive reading in church.[10] Like the focus of attention upon political developments that are dramatic but have no effect upon well-being, banal political discourse carries assurance that people are involved in fateful or significant events.

These observations are manifestly not intended to suggest that all political arguments are equally valid or invalid. The point, rather, is that social situations and discourses create political arguments that cannot be finally verified or falsified. As a society, multiple realities and relative standards are all we ever achieve.

The largely technical and specialized language that directly activates resource allocations as part of the administrative actions of governments and corporations is inevitably responsive to established social inequalities, for this form of policy making minimizes public attention and maximizes bargaining among directly interested groups that come to know each other's resources well.[11] In the making of such decisions there is direct,

10. George Orwell, "Politics and the English Language," in *A Collection of Essays* (Garden City: Doubleday-Anchor, 1954), 172.

11. Hugh Heclo, "Issue Networks and the Executive Establishment," in *The New American Political System,* ed. Anthony King (Washington, D.C.: American Enterprise Institute, 1978), 87–124.

though unequal, participation by those who can bargain while the publicized activities of government amount largely to a ritual of vicarious participation that is a necessary prelude to public acquiescence in implementing decisions.

To examine the stylized utterances of public officials, interest group spokespersons, and concerned citizens as they interact on a topic of common concern is to be impressed with the cogency of Michel Foucault's insight that there is an important sense in which language constructs the people who use it,[12] a view manifestly in contrast with the commonsensical assumption that people construct the language they use. For every political problem and ideological dilemma there is a set of statements and expressions constantly in use. In accepting one or another of these texts a person becomes a particular kind of subject with a particular ideology, role, and self-conception: a liberal or a conservative, a victim of authority or a supporter of authority, an activist or a spectator. But the choice among available language forms is itself constrained rather than free. The Secretary of Agriculture is not free to declare that wages should be higher in relation to farm income. Police chiefs are expected to focus on the importance of maintaining law and order rather than on the anarchic virtues of disorder. Employers whose plants are being picketed in labor disputes do not express their enthusiasm for strong unions.

The public interested in an issue is able to choose among a small set of stock texts that everyone who grows up in a particular culture learns early: poverty as the fault of the poor or of social institutions; abortion as a form of freedom or a form of murder; and so on. For people in a particular social situation there is sometimes only one socially viable option. In every such situation the appropriate and inappropriate forms of expression are clear to all who are involved, even while their choice of the appropriate form defines those who use it as particular kinds of people.

In the arts, by contrast, the range of discourses appropriate for use is wide, and inventiveness is socially encouraged by influential clients of the arts. Idiosyncrasy and avant garde forms become

12. *Cf.* Michel Foucault, *The Order of Things* (New York: Partheon Books 1971); *The Archeology of Knowledge* (New York: Harper & Row, 1976). A similar idea appears in the works of other twentieth century European social theorists, notably in Heidegger, Lacan, Derrida, and Ricoeur.

controversial, but there are linguistic and social bases for their survival and, occasionally, their ultimate general acceptance. Such supportive texts are an inherent part of what "art" means. In politics, however, the condition essential for success is support or acquiescence of a substantial part of the public rather than only an avant garde minority. The endorsement of a minority that symbolizes extremism, an avant garde, or an original perspective that defies conventional ideologies becomes a kiss of death rather than a signal of creativity. To maintain adequate support and acquiescence aspirants for political leadership and for social acceptance must choose from a circumscribed set of banal texts.

The more successful aspirants may find felicitous phrases or nonverbal postures in which to express their positions, and their stylistic inventiveness is easily confused with substantive creativity. A sensitive catalogue of the stylistic felicities of William Jennings Bryan, Franklin Roosevelt, Winston Churchill, John Kennedy, Adolf Hitler, Ronald Reagan, and other political leaders celebrated for their language skills would probably also reveal a small pattern of forms that appeal to large audiences. Their most celebrated phrases become banal when paraphrased in ordinary language. When Roosevelt offered hope to a despairing country in the depths of the Great Depression with the phrase, "All we have to fear is fear itself," he was taking the role any president is constrained to take in such a situation and paraphrasing the pollyannaish optimism of Herbert Hoover's phrase, "Prosperity is just around the corner." Both of them were wrong, it turned out, though that is incidental to the point. The leader of a country in imminent danger of aggression from a foreign enemy is expected to assure the population that resistance will be resolute, and Churchill did that in 1940 in his "We will fight them on the beaches . . ." speech. It is not creativity that wins an audience in such cases, but rather telling people what they want to hear in a context that makes the message credible. Hoover undermined the credibility of his optimism by denying that the depression was serious or that the federal government needed to act. FDR affirmed both these propositions while offering the same optimism. The political reality that language helps evoke depends heavily upon context, but has no necessary bearing on the realities constructed in other contexts or at later times. It has even less bearing on the creativity of speakers or audiences.

The language of promises that desired political goals will be reached similarly illustrates the sense in which language constructs what people experience as their subjectivity. Political language consists very largely of promises about the future benefits that will flow from whatever cause, policy, or candidate the writer or speaker favors. Promises of peace, prosperity, and other inversions of current fears win support for actions portrayed as the avenues to this brighter future. These "means" consist very largely of unequal sacrifices in the present: cuts in social benefits, restrictions on civil liberties, unemployment, taxes, military drafts, and wars.

The promises are bits of language always available for use; they create subjects who are bemused with a stock "other": a leader on earth or in heaven; a vision of a utopia or a dystopia; a devotion or an antipathy to a cause; an attachment to a form of rationality. To take the role of such an "other" constructed by language is to shape the meanings of observations and of other language in a determinate way. Observations become relevant and significant in the light of the self-definition of the subject. For followers and admirers of the current President, a decline in inflation rates is due to his beneficent policies. For his antagonists, the same drop is attributable to economic policies that brought a high level of unemployment and economic decline. It is not facts or observations that are critical, but rather language that constructs observers in various social situations as particular kinds of subjects.

The definition of a claim or a statement as meaningful reflects and reinforces an ideology, a subject, and a reality. Those who accept electoral contests between Republicans and Democrats as the paramount influence upon value allocations, for example, construct a world in which class, race, sex and other inequalities are not paramount and in which electoral promises are descriptions of the future rather than rationalizations of current inequalities. Those who see a profound distinction between the terms "authoritarian" and "totalitarian" as characterizations of contemporary regimes construct a world in which some deprivations of human rights are therapeutic and others are evil and in which subjects who fail to accept this distinction are dupes while those who accept it are insightful and patriotic. To name the leaders (or "ringleaders") in an uprising, refer to forced recruitment by either side in a third world civil war, or take a survey of voting intentions is to help legitimize one moral posture and implicitly help refute a contrary one. Language, subjectivity, and realities define one another; and this performative function of language is all the more potent in politics when it is masked, presenting itself as a tool for objective description. Ideological argument through a dramaturgy of objective description may be the most common gambit in political language usage.

Political Language as Deconstruction

A clear understanding of political language as social interaction emerges from an examination of the ways such language systematically undermines its own premises. In the last several decades such poststructuralist writers as Jacques Derrida and Paul de Man have sensitized us to the lessons that can be learned from the deconstruction of literary texts and critical writing. The deconstruction of political language is revealing because contradiction, ambivalence, and an endless horizon of signs that evoke each other are integral to political action and are typically displayed more naively in political texts than in more sophisticated writing.

Deconstructive analysis reveals in the starkest way the truth of Kenneth Burke's observation that political rhetoric serves to "sharpen up the pointless and blunt the too sharply pointed."[13] Political language can win or maintain public support or acquiescence in the face of other actions that violate moral qualms and typically does so by denying the premises on which such actions are based while retaining traces of the premises.

The most compelling way, then, in which political language undermines itself is through its inversions of the value hierarchies implicit in the actions and in the other language with which it is associated. To wage war is to foster peace. Capital punishment is a means to curb violence. The grant of rate increases and monopolies to public utilities is regulation. Inhibition of the autonomy of the poor, the young, and the distressed is "helping." Denial of benefits to the indigent is promotion of self-reliance and independence. And so on. Both liberal and conservative policies and rhetoric are replete with such inversions in naming what governmental action accomplishes.

13. Kenneth Burke, *A Grammar of Motives* (New York: Prentice-Hall, 1945), 393.

The language in which public officials, aspirants to office, and interest groups appeal for support, the preambles to statutes, court *obiter dicta*, and popular discussions of public issues can be understood as affirmations waiting to be ignored, qualified, or accepted according to the unknowable situations in which people find themselves at later times. While this feature is self-evident in the language of everyone's political opponents, it masks its own presence in the language of politicians one likes, thereby performing still another inversion.

Such value inversions do not necessarily signal hypocrisy. They reveal, rather, the openness of language to varying situations and to the range of interests of speakers and audiences, regardless of conventional logic. They may reflect the imperatives of new situations, or they may be evidence that life and politics are absurd.

This perspective rejects the common view that there is some ultimate foundation of language, experience, and ideas: a fundamental origin such as God, reason, or the self. Jacques Derrida calls the latter position "logocentrism," and his work tries to combat its influence upon Western philosophy.

Political language deconstructs itself in other ways as well. Political actions that, from one perspective, are self-serving or based upon the exploitation of vulnerable groups of people are invariably justified in appeals to reason, objectivity, and detachment; and there is always a sense in which both positions are valid and can be demonstrated "rationally."

Deconstruction proceeds as well through the use of adverbial or adjectival qualifiers that purport at one level of meaning to intensify an affirmation while they negate it at another level. The most general qualifiers are synonyms of "essential" or "true" as modifiers of words like "freedom," "democracy," "justice," or "communism." The speaker who advocates "true" freedom is invariably arguing for restraints on some group's freedom, just as the insertion of the word "true" before "equality" is a sign that some inequality is being rationalized. The lyncher sees vigilante violence as true justice. The liberal sees a choice between two centrist and ambiguous candidates as true participation while a radical sees the same procedure as self-deception. In these and similar cases language offers a logic to defend any position regardless of contradictions, and it does so subtly.

There are constant claims that policies to deal with the social problems that are never solved (poverty, crime, inflation, unemployment, emotional disturbance, and so on) are failures and also that they are successes; each claim is a necessary supplement to the contradictory one and is made because the other is made. Each such problem, moreover, is regularly defined in different statements both as personal pathology and as social pathology, contradictory premises that are also closely linked to the conflicting claims about success and failure. Language about the most persistent problems governments face may be experienced as analysis or as description, but can also be recognized as a proliferating chain of texts that are grafted onto each other, providing supplementary and contradictory rationalizations for courses of action.

Underlying all the forms of deconstruction that political language exhibits is play upon the various associations of terms, thereby reassuring speakers of their own integrity and attracting support from people who would not otherwise be concerned with the issue. This device, which is sometimes deliberate but more often employed unconsciously, relies upon the characteristics of language that Derrida calls the "trace" and the "graft." To speak or hear a term is to experience the spoor of other terms. Language therefore entails a wide range of resonances that are both present and absent, available for recognition and also for denial. Like much of Derrida's work, this perspective challenges conventional logic and the conventional centering of thought in the subject (rather than in the text), yet it recognizes what we know to be the case and encourages us to analyze language incisively.

The traces of political terms make it easy to link issues in dubious and challengeable ways, and such grafting is endemic in political discourse. A racist or sexist practice can be linked to the issue of states' rights. Protection of the health of workers bears the aura of bureaucratic intervention in a private matter. The possibilities are limitless and so, therefore, are the practices, the responses, and the controversial exchange of terms. Because the conventional analysis of such debates turns on claims about the validity of the problematic linkages, we conventionally fail to notice that the characteristics of language as aspects of specific social situations constitute the issues and the arguments and make it likely that they will not be resolved.

The failure to resolve or solve political problems is a paramount characteristic of government, though regimes have an obvious interest in claiming successes, and there is always support for denying an observation that challenges the conventional assumptions that political beliefs are rational and that governmental actions in some sense reflect the public will.

It might be claimed that governments have solved some social problems and therefore can be expected to continue to do so. Slavery has been abolished, for example, and universal education has been established in the United States, ending two major problems that dominated political debate in the first half of the nineteenth century. These examples do demonstrate that the terms in which the problems are named have been transformed. But the deprivations, inequalities, and moral questions that made them issues in the first place have remained as major items on the political agenda, with no resolution in sight. The problem of black slavery has become the problem of race and minority relations. The problem of inadequate education for the masses has remained an incorrigible one, though the terms in which it is discussed are now social or economic rather than legal. In each case legal action has erased a legal issue, but not a complex of social and economic issues. This is almost certainly an improvement, but it also raises false hopes. The point could be made about other problems as well that the language in which they are debated has been transformed while many of the deprivations that constitute the problems persist in old or new forms.

The industrial revolution and the growth of capitalist industry in America in the first half of the nineteenth century made wage labor more economical than slave labor (workers could be fired when not needed and did not have to be supported in old age) and also created a need for a literate and disciplined labor force, so that public schooling that taught literacy, conformity, and discipline became a necessity, especially as it was supported by regressive taxation. The rhetoric of freedom from involuntary servitude and of universal free education enjoyed a certain validity as heralding greater democracy while also legitimizing a major benefit for the owners of large amounts of capital.

These deconstructions of political language are not evidence that it is corrupt or nonsensical. On the contrary, they demonstrate that social life and the human brain are more subtle and meaningful than either common sense or conventional social science analysis suggests. Every term and every entity in the environment is a signifier, and signifiers evoke a range of meanings that continue to widen endlessly. It is evident that the dominant meanings rationalize existing social inequalities, but always in ways that subvert those values and premises as well.

While language, consciousness, and social conditions are replete with contradictions, they shape each other to make it possible for people to live with themselves, with their moral dilemmas, and with chronic failure to resolve the dilemmas and the contradictions.

7 The Political Spectacle as Tactic and as Mystification

News about politics encourages a focus upon leaders, enemies, and problems as sources of hope and of fear, obscuring the sense in which they are creations of discourse, perpetuators of ideologies, and facets of a single transaction. A strategy for analyzing politics as spectacle must begin with language that highlights the controversial perspectives inherent in these terms and calls attention to the social formations they conceal.

They help to politicize the public and so keep it both apprehensive and hopeful. They evoke a dramatic setting that impinges upon private lives: a scene comprised of effective and ineffective leaders managing the effort to cope with distressing problems and to defend the polity against external and internal enemies. The evocation helps erase history, social structure, economic inequalities, and discourse from the schemas that account for well-being and privations. These concepts may also confound individual and group strategies for influencing the course of public affairs.

Other common terms reinforce these effects by displacing public and scholarly attention from the construction of political spectacles to a factual political scene composed of autonomous elements that interact with one another as causes, consequences, origins, targets, allies, and antagonists. Spectators grow bemused with the interactions among such entities and remain oblivious to the sense in which they take their meaning from an ideologically constructed political world. Reported political language and other actions foster the bemusement and obliviousness.

The effects are powerful because these constructions offer answers to troubling questions. They tell what conditions are healthy or threatening and who are responsible for success and for misfortune. The answers are the more salient because alternative and contradictory ones press for acceptance as well, a phenomenon that transforms every acceptance or rejection into a challenge and a self-definition. A focus upon leaders, problems, and enemies accordingly constructs a social world that justifies the observer's role, status and actions and also makes contradictory claims understandable.

The constructions are explanations, though parochial ones, but they are also provocations that perpetuate political tensions, conflicts, and maneuverings for advantage that can never succeed for long. For some people it is gratifying to postulate a world with the particular contours they construct; its components are logically consistent with each other and so contribute to understanding, to prediction, and to control within the postulated parameters. A world, for example, in which rebellions and civil wars in third world countries are aspects of the conflict between the United States and the Soviet Union generates clear beliefs about who are virtuous and who are evil, which leaders are on which side, which social problems are real, which alleged problems, such as peasant repression and poverty, are propaganda, and which courses of action are well advised. Alternative worlds may generate beliefs that are inversions of those just outlined. Either set can be a welcome explanation for the course of public affairs and either perpetuates and aggravates the political tensions it explains.

As suggested in chapter 1, it does not follow that any such construction is as good as any other as an explanation or a recipe for action. Some may be based on valid premises and reasoning and others on wishful thinking or on delusions; but all are interventions into the political scene they purport to explain, for they encourage actions that exacerbate tensions.

The Spectacle as a Single Transaction

Problems, leaders, and enemies are alternative perspectives from which to view a single transaction. In order to understand each of them it has been necessary to consider the many ways they evoke and complement each other. Problems create authorities to deal with them, and the threats they name are often personified as enemies. Leaders achieve and maintain their positions by focusing upon fashionable or feared problems and by emphasizing their differences from enemies whose past and potential sins they publicize and exaggerate. Enemies are a vivid aspect of problems and a source of the differences that construct leaders.

As an influence upon the public and upon politics, then, there is a single reality, but it is experienced as several distinct entities.

This phenomenon is likely to enhance confidence in beliefs and judgments because each of the components of the transaction seems to provide independent evidence, even if their autonomy is illusory. The seeming independence of leaders, problems, and enemies offers advocates of causes alternative ways of focusing public attention: diverse narratives with a common implication.

A focus, for example, upon large fiscal deficits as a problem may define liberal spenders on social programs and those who benefit from those programs as the enemy and construct an official who slashed social programs as a leader. Such a construction seems to rest upon three discrete elements that reinforce its ideological thrust, but they are part of a common structure of beliefs. The example calls attention as well to the crucial role of interpretation because the same fiscal deficit can also define defense spenders as the enemy; or, as in the case of Franklin Roosevelt, the deficit can be interpreted as a solution rather than a problem.

The Diverse Media

The ramifications of news reports for political ideology have grown in importance with the advent in the last century of widespread literacy in the industrialized countries and of radio and television in much of the populated world. Because more minds can be reached, governments and interest groups try harder to reach them.

The various media attract rather different audiences according to level of education, social class, ideology, age, interests, and other influences. The specialized appeals of magazines and journals are especially clear. Radio stations also appeal to specific publics, at least so far as musical taste and sometimes ethnic and political interests are concerned. Radio and television programs are designed to attract specific audiences, and the same is true of newspaper features.

While these differences in appeal create an impression of pluralistic diversity, the key process at work is observer selectivity and the construction of their own spectacles by groups with common interests. The chief result is a reinforcement of established ideologies that is all the more potent because it takes place in a context that highlights diverse stimuli.

Political Stability and the Acceptance of Authority

Political history chronicles a great deal of frustration and tragedy, and people acquiesce in the frustration and tragedy without resistance most of the time. Plans, policies, strategies, and revolutions promising a happier social world have never worked for many or for long and have often made things worse. The classic question about politics is why large numbers of people support the authority of governments that require acceptance of that kind of history and obedience to onerous rules.

In the contemporary world, spectacle construction is an important part of the answer because the contriving of events and the dissemination of news about them create anxieties and aspirations, insecurities and reassurances, that fuel a search for legitimating symbols. Rejection of authority is seldom without costs, but it would be a lot more common if political news did not keep people both continuously anxious and constantly hopeful. Exposure to the news involves the public in a world of surprises and drama. Defeats and triumphs, unexpected threats and gratifying victories, fears of profound changes in well-being, and hopes for the end of worrisome problems make news reports intriguing for some and the future uncertain for all. The spectacle is unpredictable and fragmented, so that individuals are always vulnerable and usually can do little more than react, chiefly by keeping abreast of the news that concerns them and by acquiescing in the realities it creates.

Interpretation as Explanation

This tour of the stances from which people construct political spectacles deals in uncertainties, interpretations, and contradictions, not in conclusive generalizations. Political understanding lies in awareness of the range of meanings political phenomena present and in appreciation of their potentialities for generating change in actions and beliefs. It does not spring from designating some one interpretation as fact, truth, or scientific finding.

The social philosophies that remain vital near the end of the twentieth century see "covering laws" and definitive answers as misleading rather than scientific: as rationalizations for exalting the dominant interpretations by giving them the status of science. These philosophies focus instead upon the central importance of variation in experience with the social situation, the form of discourse, and the context, perspective, and definition of the whole transaction of which any observation is a part. They sensitize us as well to the inevitability of distortion in expression and in understanding because of efforts to say things that cannot be said, the radiation of signifiers and of traces of other signifiers, and the sense in which texts undermine their own premises. Rather than verifiability or falsifiability and the certainties and dogmatisms to which the search for definitive answers leads, a useful analysis must examine the consequences of uncertainties, unjustified certainties, the variations in response that diverse social milieus evoke, and the potentiality for multivalent responses to situations and to texts.

The historian or social scientist who self-consciously looks for stability in political developments can find it as readily as the general public finds the drama and the surprises *it* expects. While the labels for enemies and for threats and the names of leaders and reassurances change from time to time, their consequences for daily life and for well-being remain stable. Change in content keeps the form and its political consequences vivid.

Manifestly, there *is* social change over long time periods, catalyzed chiefly by radical, and usually slow, alterations in environment, demography, and modes of production, as Fernand Braudel demonstrated in his masterful histories of the Mediterranean and of capitalism.[1] Political and governmental actions do not initiate social change, though they reflect it and thrive upon the belief that they cause it.

What an action means depends upon the moral stance from which it is observed. Some of the interpretations in this book flow from the assumption that equality in benefits and in harm from the outcomes of public policies is ordinarily desirable; but much of the book suggests that the constructed spectacle either conceals inequalities or justifies them. Some people see that

1. Fernand Braudel, *The Mediterranean and the Mediterranean World in the Age of Philip II*, 2 vols. (New York: Harper & Row, 1966); *Capitalism and Material Life; 1400–1800* (New York: Harper & Row, 1967).

result of spectacle construction as distortion while others do not because they approve of the consequences. Normative judgments and observations are inextricably intertwined.

The privileged benefit more than the disadvantaged from spectacle construction, as many of the examples and conclusions in earlier chapters illustrate. By definition a spectacle highlights the obtrusive current news that captures its audience and seems to have a self-evident meaning. The meaning and the development itself are typically expressions and vivid reinforcements of the dominant ideology that justifies extant inequalities. They divert attention from historical knowledge, social and economic analysis and unequal benefits and sufferings that might raise questions about prevailing ideology. A journalistic account of welfare cheating is a more potent political weapon than a scholarly analysis of the causes of poverty and of the pressures, terrors, and lack of options the poor can face.

Do officials and elites intentionally take advantage of the processes examined here to maintain and improve their privileges? They sometimes do so quite self-consciously, but conspiracies and scheming are not nearly as useful in maintaining inequalities as the more pervasive actions that flow from the logic of the social situations in which people find themselves. Elites take advantage of the resources available to them, and most support the institutions that allocate resources unequally because their situations make those courses of action look rational. Intentions are likely to be confused and ambivalent. To define them is itself a political act that flows from the situation and the language forms available to observers. Explanation is more adequate when it deals in actions, structural conditions and consequences than when it deals in the attribution of intentions.

The very construction of the spectacle through the daily acts of officials and interest groups illustrates that point. In one sense they cope with problems, threats, and opportunities as they carry on the processes of government; but every action also helps construct beliefs about their status as leaders, allies, adversaries, or enemies and about the relevance or irrelevance of their acts for particular audiences. The construction of a spectacle and everyday political action are the same thing, though the pretence that they are separate helps legitimize official actions.

Antidotes

For most of the human race political history has been a record of the triumph of mystification over strategies to maximize well-being. This book deals chiefly in ineffective strategies because the political efforts of most of the population go into them.

Though it is not often successful for many or for extended time periods, art is worth attention as an antidote to political mystification because works of art depend for their power upon properties that contrast revealingly with the characteristics of political language. Art helps counter banal political forms and so can be a liberating form of political expression. It becomes that when it estranges people from bemusement with facts, conventional assumptions, and conventional language so that they see their inherent contradictions and recognize alternative potentialities.

Political language is rooted in the present, fixing attention upon current "realities" and upon promises to change them in the future to solve contemporary problems; but such means-end language is a buttress of conventional assumptions, as noted earlier.[2] The facts with which it begins are valid only in the light of those assumptions; "verification" of the facts reinforces the same premises, stifling analysis and imagination. The individual caught in a cycle of reported developments, political promises, and actions that minimize choice needs an estranged perspective from which to analyze the cycle.

There has been some fruitful exploration of the sense in which art refuses to accept fact as truth and so liberates the mind from conventional presuppositions. The distinctive properties of artistic symbolism are crucial. In a recent book Nelson Goodman listed five "symptoms of the aesthetic" that include: syntactic density, semantic density, comparative repleteness ("where comparatively many aspects of a symbol are significant"), and multiple complex reference.[3] His emphasis, then, is upon complex associations and dense meanings as the hallmarks of the aesthetic. While political language focuses attention upon

2. See chapter 6.
3. Nelson Goodman, *Ways of Worldmaking* (Indianapolis: Hacket Publishing Co., 1978), 67–68.

a particular fear or a hope, art evokes many concurrent levels of significance. The work of the Frankfurt School and of such aesthetic theorists as Langer[4] and Lukács[5] point in the same direction. Art provides significant form,[6] and Bertolt Brecht linked the destruction of form to banality.

Consider conceptions of crime in everyday life and in art as an illustration of the distinction. To a politician advocating a tougher stance toward criminals, to a criminologist studying the causes of crime, and to a journalist reporting a particular murder, the person who kills is defined by his or her act and represents a known role, a common threat, and a justification for conventional policies. To the reader of *Crime and Punishment* Raskolnikov represents these things and others, but also their negations. Among other possibilities he represents the anguish of poverty, the confused thinking of victims and of beneficiaries of an unfair society, the confounding pressures of obligations to family and to self, the horror felt by a person who acts in one state of mind and regrets the action in another. Dostoevsky's detailed exploration of Raskolnikov's world and mind makes of him a universal that transcends temporal, spatial, national, and sociological limits.

The pessimism that characterizes much of the greatest art and the humor that is often intermixed with pessimism help to counter political language as well. Pessimism in art is a component of its humanizing power; it offers a liberating contrast to the rosy promises with which political and commercial pitchmen assault the public. Marcuse sees it as a useful antidote of the optimism of radicals as well:

Compared with the often one-dimensional optimism of propaganda, art is permeated with pessimism, not seldom intertwined with comedy. Its liberating laughter recalls the danger and the evils that have passed—this time! But the pessimism of art is not counterrevolutionary. It serves to warn against the 'happy consciousness' of radical praxis: as if all of that which art invokes and indicts could be settled through the class struggle.[7]

4. Suzanne Langer, *Philosophy in a New Key* (Cambridge: Harvard University Press, 1970).
5. Georg Lukács, *The Specific Nature of the Aesthetic*, excerpted in *Marxism and Art*, ed. Maynard Solomon (New York: Knopf, 1973) 404–19.
6. Suzanne Langer, *Feeling and Form* (New York: Scribner, 1953).
7. Herbert Marcuse, *The Aesthetic Dimension* (Boston: Beacon Press, 1978), 14.

Though humor in art is less likely to elicit profound under-standing of the distortions of propaganda, it has an immediate appeal and more direct political consequences than pessimism. The popular humor that calls attention to the special subculture that binds disadvantaged people to one another can be powerful. In an essay on Rabelais, Mikhail Bakhtin saw the focus of medieval lower class people on drinking, screwing, birth, eating, and defecation as a form of opposition to social inequality. The point doubtless applies in other eras as well, for laughter about such matters distances people from the official culture that is serious, repressive, and authoritarian. Bakhtin wrote:

Laughter liberates not only from external censorship but first of all from the great interior censor; it liberates from the fear that developed in man during thousands of years: fear of the sacred, of prohibitions, of the past, of power . . . Laughter opened men's eyes on that which is new, on the future . . . This is why laughter could never become an instrument to oppress and blind people. It always remained a free weapon in their hands.[8]

These observations about a form of expression that contrasts fundamentally with political communication help us understand the latter, and they say something as well about the possibility of individual emancipation from the mystifications of politics. Waves of collective resistance to repression have always been encouraged by works of art that helped illuminate the possi-bilities for action and for conceptualization: paintings, dance, novels, films, theater, and some forms of popular culture.

Perspectives that distance people from involvement in con-ventional ideologies have been an occasional theme of these pages, and works of art are a paramount vehicle for such dis-tancing. Collective resistance is itself a catalyst of an estranged perspective. The distancing is typically short-lived because it is only one moment among a plethora of stronger ones that work against it, but it is significant in itself and a valuable concomitant of political action.

More generally, a potential for liberation from political texts and their rootedness in the present lies in the refusal to see any text or any form of discourse as paramount or essential; it lies in sensitivity to the multiple and contradictory realities and the

8. Solomon, *Marxism and Art*, 300.

occasional transformations of reality associated with changed discourses, diverse social situations, and different historical contexts.

Such sensitivity is rare and is difficult to achieve and maintain, though there have been historical moments when large numbers of people have achieved it. Challengers of the dominant order try to promote it through "counterdiscourses:"[9] texts that challenge hegemony by undermining its presuppositions and offering alternatives. This tactic has occasionally worked for some for a time, though the very success of a particular counterdiscourse may buttress hegemony by constructing a stable enemy or threat that justifies authority, as noted earlier.[10] Emancipatory language does not focus on a specific alternative but rather builds an appreciation of the range of discourses, perspectives, and political realities: the diverse realities that go with immediate involvement and with self-conscious distancing; with synchronic analysis and with attention to history; with a passive posture and with struggle; with differences in class, gender, color, and ethnicity; with the constructions of art, science, political actions, and fantasy. Understanding the range of perspectives from which people constitute their worlds implies a critical posture. The writings of Max Weber on *Verstehen*[11] and of Alfred Schutz on existential phenomenology[12] offer some confidence that it is feasible to understand a range of positions without subscribing to them. Such a stance makes it possible to plan concerted and effective action by taking the roles of the spectrum of significant actors. On occasion it may mean adopting forms of language and action that are strategic at the time but would be unrealistic or counterproductive in a different social situation.

This position implies that political struggles can succeed only partially and temporarily: it excludes a final state of fairness or utopia as a goal and as an ideal. Utopian writings can reinforce hope and contribute to useful practice and theory, especially

---

9. For a perceptive analysis of counterdiscourses in nineteenth-century French literature see Richard Terdiman, *Discourse/Counterdiscourse* (Ithaca: Cornell University Press, 1985).

10. See "The Creation of Difference and Opposition in Leaders," Chapter 3.

11. Max Weber, *The Methodology of the Social Sciences* (New York: The Free Press, 1949).

12. Alfred Schutz, *The Phenomenology of the Social World* (Evanston, Il: Northwestern University Press, 1967).

when they take account of institutionalized resistances to change; but reveries about an idealized future more often root people in the present, inverting whatever the writer dislikes about the contemporary social order and buttressing an optimism that history belies. Like language promising that one or another political cause will remedy discontents, such reveries rationalize acquiescence in the actual.

Direct political action through voting and lobbying can help bring modest and temporary changes, but are more effective as psychological balm for those who engage in them than as agencies of lasting and significant change, because the very focus upon politics in a narrow sense takes the existing institutional framework for granted and so reinforces it.

Though this analysis pays a great deal of attention to language, change in language is not a final answer either. The dissemination of new political terms, concepts, and phrases without concomitant change in material conditions can only reinforce the old tensions and premises. Awareness of the long odds against substantial change may help shape effective strategies, especially if it is coupled with recognition that art, science, and culture construct political thought and action rather than simply coexisting with them.

Decisive change requires struggle based on hope, but even struggle that disrupts established institutions, routines, and assumptions has not often been effective for long. Analysis of the nature and consequences of the spectacle of politics is itself a part of the ongoing struggle.

Index

Adversaries. *See* Enemies; Political adversaries

Affect, political, sources of, 39

Ambiguity: of claims, in public problem-solving, 15–16; for enemies, 71–72, 74, 81; incentive to reduce to certainty, 3–4; in leadership, 37, 38, 41–42, 50, 63; of news accounts, 91, 95, 100–101; and opinions, 19; in political developments, 1–2, 15, 25, 54, 63, 85; in political language, 38, 104–5, 110–11, 115 (*see also* Political language, incoherence of); Roosevelt's use of, 57; and social problems, 15–17

Ambivalence, 15, 33, 59, 71–72, 74, 80, 81

America. *See* United States

American Indians, 13, 87

Antidotes, art as, 126–28. *See also* Solutions

Apathy, political, 6–9, 33–34

Appeal, and political aspirants, 63

Arendt, Hannah, 43–44

Art, and politics, 4, 112–13, 126–28

Assumptions, in political language, 126

Audience: as creators of public problems, 32–34; and news, 99–101

Authority: constitution of, 20–21, 121–22; of leaders, 12, 38–39; rejection of, 123

Bachrach, Peter, 13

Bakhtin, Mikhail, 128

Banality: of evil, in state functions, 89, 111, 127; and mass communication, 40

Bay of Pigs, 41, 58

Beliefs, evoked by political language, 105

Bentley, Arthur, 45

Bemusement, and reported political language, 120

Blame, 64, 78–80, 89

Botha, P. W., 48

Braudel, Fernand, 124

Brecht, Bertolt, 127

Brezhnev, Leonid, 63

Bryan, William Jennings, 113

Bumiller, Kristin, 26

Bureaucratic domination, 54–56, 85

Burke, Kenneth, 115

Burns, James McGregor, 46–47, 48

Caesar, Julius, 47

Camp David peace talks, 42

"Capital punishment," as condensation symbol, 73

Carlyle, Thomas, 44–45

Carter, Jimmy, 41

Central America, 76

Chauvinism, and leadership, 61–62. *See also* Father image

China, 71

Choice, among political aspirants, 62–64

Chomsky, Noam, 107

Churchill, Winston, 56, 113

Coalitions, political, 68–70

Cognitive structuring, and enemy construction, 80–82

Cointel project, Nixon administration, 79

Collective resistance, 128

Condensation symbol, 22, 70, 73

Conformity, of leaders to followers, 37–38

"Consciousness industry," in politics, 7–8

Consensus: in political developments, 2–3, 18–19, 104–5; of social practices, 14

131